*Room in
Her Head*

Room in Her Head

A Guide for Men on Women's Mental Load,
How It Affects Sexual Desire,
and What to Do About It

Dr. Celeste McClannahan

Dr. Celeste Press
Stanwood, Washington

Published by Dr. Celeste Press
Stanwood, Washington
info@drceleste.life
www.drceleste.life

Dr. Celeste Press books are available at special quantity discounts for bulk purchase for sales promotions, events, fundraising, and educational needs. Special books or book excerpts also can be created to fit specific needs. For details and permission requests, write to the email address above.

ISBN 979-8-9989065-1-0 (eBook)
ISBN 979-8-9989065-0-3 (paperback)
ISBN 979-8-9989065-2-7 (hardback)

10 9 8 7 6 5 4 3 2 1

—

Copyediting by James Gallagher
Proofreading by Adeline Hull
Book Design & Publishing by Kory Kirby
SET IN LIBRE BASKERVILLE

I dedicate this work to my faithfully supportive husband.

Without his encouragement,
I would not have been able to finish.

Contents

Acknowledgments

I would like to acknowledge my appreciation of Dr. Eric Amsel, my mentor, friend, and chair of my doctoral committee who has supported me since I began my journey with psychology in 2013. Throughout my doctoral journey, he guided me through the process of writing this book for couples.

Thank you, also, to Dr. Susan Raab-Cohen for joining in this process with me. You are a wonderful friend and mentor. Both doctors contributed their experience and knowledge, which were highly influential in creating this for men and women.

Introduction

You just don't get it! As a man, how often have you heard this kind of statement from your wife or partner, said in exasperation when you are trying to be helpful? You want to be there and show up for her, but she gets upset and you don't understand why she is so frustrated. It seems like it is more complex than what you take to be a simple issue. Where is the complexity coming from, and why can't she just explain it to you so you get it? It isn't like you are trying to be obstinate on purpose, and it seems like she is making life harder than it needs to be. Why does she do that to herself? This book lets you in to the complexity so you can understand why she gets frustrated. Then you can actually know what to do to improve your relationship.

This book is written to men in heterosexual relationships, mainly because my research has shown that people in homosexual relationships do not struggle with mental load and sexual desire in the same way that people in heterosexual relationships do.[1] This book will help a man understand

---

[1 Macedo et al., 2023.

what his partner is talking about when she is saying she is exhausted and he doesn't get it. Of course, anyone can read this book and learn from it, but the people I am speaking to are men in heterosexual relationships who do not understand what mental load is and do not understand why their partners are so tired at night and don't want to have sex. For anyone, though, if it fills a need for you, that is great, and please read on.

Understanding Mental Load (the Secret!)

In my practice working with couples on strengthening their relationships, I hear all the time that he doesn't get it, and then he shares that he is trying, but it never seems to be good enough. When I hear this, I help couples see each other from their partners' experience instead of through their own, which builds understanding, compassion, and empathy toward each other. When couples begin to do this, they develop a fresh, safe, and secure relationship, and they improve their communication so they can share anything, navigate challenges more smoothly, and feel stronger within the new relationship.

We are going to address things that are invisible and occur so quietly in the background you may not even know all the work that is happening before physical labor even takes place. When she says that she is too emotionally or mentally exhausted at the end of the day to even have sex, you are going to understand what that means. By the end, you will even know what to do to help with that invisible labor so she is not so exhausted and might still have energy left for sex.

What am I talking about? It is the unpaid, domestic, invisible, caring, emotional, mental labor that women largely carry and men rarely notice—or are even aware of its existence. This mental load can become overwhelming because it feels like she has to carry it alone or no one will carry it. She suffers silently, wishing with all her soul that you would share this burden and partner with her to get things done. She wants to feel that you are not just another person for her to take care of, that you stand beside her, sharing the load of caring for everyone, and that you have each other's backs.

How Did I Get Here?

I used to have people come to me to share life experiences all the time. I can remember sitting on a bench in a park, watching my children play, and having strangers sit next to me. After a few minutes, I would know what they were dealing with, as they felt safe to share with me. This happened multiple times in various locations, and I decided to get my master's degree in therapy and make a career out of this drive to help people. Over the past five years, I have worked with more than one hundred couples, and my biggest joy is when they graduate from couples therapy, because they then feel safe and secure in their relationship.

Basic Structure of This Book

There will be reflections throughout the book that you can choose to stop and think through. The purpose of these reflections is to help you slow down and make sure you are taking in the information (and not just reading without internalizing). You could do these on your own, or you could do the reflections and then talk them through with your partner to bring about meaningful conversation that might provide more clarity.

To help describe what I am talking about, I will use a couple and their stories throughout the book. This couple is fictional, but their stories are a compilation of stories from couples in my office, from friends and family, and even from my own relationships. The stories illustrate how the things we are discussing play out in relationships and daily life.

Let's Meet our Couple

Sandy and Mark have been together for ten years with three- and five-year-old boys. Mark runs a business out of the home, and Sandy is a homemaker until the boys are both school age, at which time she plans to return to work again. They are struggling with communication issues and have not had sex in at least six months because "she is never in the mood," according to Mark.

> SANDY: I am just exhausted mentally and physically from chasing after our extremely active and rambunctious boys all day and trying to keep up on the "millions of things" needed to keep the family and home functional.

> MARK: (Looks at Sandy, frustrated.) I don't understand why it is so hard to be at home all day, as I also work

full-time, but I still want to have sex with you, so you simply must not find me attractive anymore.

SANDY: (Looks at Mark, sadly.) You just don't understand.

This couple is not alone. Many couples struggle with similar issues and have similar conversations, so if it sounds familiar, that is okay. As a couples therapist, I hear it in various ways in my office every day. The first thing to recognize is that this is not *her* problem; this is *their* problem. They are both contributing to the problem in their own ways, and it will take both to correct their path. It is not her figuring out what is "wrong" with her and then "fixing" herself; rather, it is both of them finding the moves that push them apart and leave them feeling like the other doesn't care.

In this book we are going to focus on helping you to understand what is going on in her mind so you will be able to be aware of what your moves are that push her away from you. As the old saying goes: *You don't know what you don't know.* So let's help to be in the know, and then you can use that knowledge to make better moves in your relationship.

The first section of the book is about what the mental load actually is and then breaking it down for you so you understand why it is so important and has such a big impact on her daily mood, emotionality, and energy level. The second part of the book explains why mental load affects sexual desire and how it works. Many times, couples do not realize that mental load affects sex drive, feeling sexy, or being drawn to the other, and it is a shock to find out it plays a significant role. The last part of the book lays out the actionable steps you can take to share the mental load in the relationship and improve your intimate relationship with your partner. I include this part of the book because every time he learns about mental load, he asks her to tell him what to do or tell him how he can help, and she gets frustrated, because that is part of the mental load. So I include the answer to this question to help you get started on making changes that will be meaningful for your relationship. So are you ready to get started and feel equipped to show up differently and more positively in your relationship?

Room in
Her Head

Part I

What Is Mental Load?

Chapter 1:

What Does "Mental Load" Mean?

I mentioned that mental load is the unpaid, domestic, invisible, caring, emotional, and mental labor that women largely carry and men rarely notice or are even aware of. Maybe you have heard this phrase before but don't get what it means, and it seems like you are expected to know, so you don't want to ask. In this section we are going to go over what the mental load is so you can get a clear picture to help you understand your partner better. The short answer is that mental load comprises excessive mental demands.[2] But what does "excessive mental demands" mean? You need more than that to get what your partner is going through.

Okay, let's start unpacking what "excessive mental demands" means and what it looks like for your partner

---

2 Díaz-García et al., 2022.

so you can notice it too. It is unseen, invisible, and unpaid labor that is necessary for managing life, and it usually goes unnoticed by everyone except the person who is doing this mental work. Surely men experience mental load, too, but the point is that the mental load that is the focus of attention is unpaid: related not to work but to domestic issues that fall disproportionately to women.

Mental load related to domestic issues is constant, meaning the time needed never decreases, and it uses a lot of emotional labor, making it heavier and more burdensome mentally than any of the other tasks that must be completed each day.[3] Before you see any physical labor being done, there is invisible labor first. Much of this invisible labor includes tasks that cover planning, remembering, delegating, and reviewing.[4] You might be wondering: What do you mean? How can something always need more time? How hard is it to think about something before doing it? It cannot possibly be that exhausting and overwhelming.

Planning

Let's start where it all starts, with planning. She is not planning for things that only she needs. It is for every member of the home, all their needs, and a way to manage it all so that it actually works. She is short-term planning and long-term planning for everyone and everything. Short-term planning is the day-to-day planning that keeps a family functional

---

3 Çevik & Wright, 2023.
4 Harrington & Reese-Melancon, 2022.

and moving forward. This includes meals, housework, phone calls, daily mini crises, and last-minute schedule changes.

For meals, this might include taking something out of the freezer in the morning so that it is defrosted by dinnertime, stopping at a grocery store to pick up an ingredient that she noticed was missing the night before, prepping things in the morning for ease throughout the day (snacks, lunches, etc.). At night it might be putting leftovers into lunch containers for easy grab-and-go for you or her the next day, thinking about what to make the next day so she knows whether she has all the ingredients or needs to make a store pickup, and prepping for anything the next day that can be done that evening.

She is taking into consideration what meals have been cooked already and what is coming up so that it does not become redundant or boring, with family members complaining that this has been made already or they just had it yesterday. She is planning based on the activities of family members to accommodate time for dinner, how long it will take to make, time for cleaning up after, and which foods will be filling but not cause them to feel sick during their activities/sports.

All that planning above was just for making dinner, which is only one part of a day, and it was only the short-term planning. There is also the planning involved in managing a home so that it runs smoothly and doesn't become an overwhelming mess, with no one knowing what is happening or should be happening. This also involves short- and long-term planning skills. In this section we are focusing on short-term planning skills. In the box below, let's try an exercise.

Write out what you think is involved in short-term planning for managing a home. (Hint: This will include anything to do with family members or the home, such as chores, tasks, activities, and schedules.)

Exercise 1.1: Short-Term Planning

Now that you have written out what you think is involved in the short-term planning for managing a home, let's dissect what she is processing while considering how her day will go. Then we will compare what you wrote out and what she includes and see what differences there are for each of you.

On her list for managing a home will be the daily tasks that need to be completed. She may use written lists, phone reminders, or a mental list to tick off as she completes items. There are always going to be the less-typical activities that require more effort than routine activities, which involve more automatic processing. She will have a list of the household chores that need to be done for that day, and many of those are everyday chores that never seem to be complete, like laundry and dishes. She may have chores that are deep-cleaning tasks that need to be completed either weekly or monthly to keep a home clean. She will be thinking about what to do for meals, what needs to be prepped, how long those tasks will take, and how to manage the time so that as much can be accomplished as possible that day. This all happens while also keeping in mind who needs to be where for what activity, and, if more than one person has an activity, then how to manage the time so no one is late, what the driving time looks like, how to get each person picked back up so that no one is forgotten or late, and what small tasks can be done between each person's activities, like taking a quick trip to the grocery store, making a meal, prepping a snack, and keeping everyone safe and healthy.[5] While thinking about the chores that need to be completed,

---

5 Pitts, 2023.

she is also processing how to do them correctly so that the chores are done well and she isn't missing steps. She has to do this because if she does not ensure that the task is done completely, then there is no one to finish it for her.

REFLECTION 1.1: Short-Term Planning Reflection Exercise (Think about these questions and reflect either in your mind or by writing in the space provided.)

What did you have on your list?

What was she thinking about?

What on your list was different from her list?

What did you realize about all the mental gymnastics that make everything work for everyone?

What was something new for you to think about?

What about long-term planning? What is involved with that part of the mental load? Usually this part involves the need for a calendar—be it digital or paper. Depending on how active the family is, this could involve the need for different colors for different people and lots of time-management skills.

When you think about long-term planning, what do you think about? Pause here and think about what it is that you believe long-term planning entails. After you reflect, look at table 1.1. This table shows some of the details of what she is managing for long-term-care items and some of the things that she holds in her mind about them. Some of these things you may know about and some you may not, so take your time to read through the table and try to take in all the details involved for each item.

LONG-TERM PLANNING ITEM	WHAT SHE DOES
School Year	• Writing down all the days off for each kid • Knowing start/end times for each day (full days / half days / late-start days) • Planning either an activity or childcare for off days (holidays / spring-winter breaks / teacher in-service days / snow days) • Signing up for chaperone activities • Ensuring registration for correct classes • Knowing dates to big activities to keep up on payments / things to buy

Kids' clothing sizes	• Setting aside time to go through what fits and what doesn't for each kid a couple of times per year • Writing down what they need now after finding out what doesn't fit • Shopping for new items that will fit • Donating / selling / trashing / setting aside for younger children items that no longer fit
Meal prepping	• Going through the pantry to see what is on hand to use what is there • Going through recipes and finding old and new recipes to mix in throughout the month (books, digital, websites) • Thinking about everyone's likes and dislikes to ensure having at least one thing on the table that will be eaten by each person • Using a calendar to see what activities are happening each night to plan the best meal that will fit the time allowed and the weight of the meal, depending on the activities and time of the meal • Writing a list for the grocery store while going through compiled recipes for the month • Shopping for groceries • Doing whatever prep can be done for each meal to make it as easy as possible for each meal

Deep cleaning of house	• Writing on the calendar each room/section/item in the house that needs to be deep cleaned each day of the month (some are weekly, some monthly) • Having a list of what it entails to deep clean each room/section/item in the house to check off as completed (some women do this mentally, and some actually write it down and check it off each time) • Ensuring the cleaning supplies for each task are on hand and adding them to the grocery list when running low to refresh the supply
Purging time	• Planning how to do yearly purging to keep the house from becoming overwhelming and full of unneeded items • Making a list (many times mentally) for each room to go through and deciding what to keep/donate/trash • Managing time to purge items that need to go to trash or donation
Activities	• Managing time for each person to go to activities and seeing what overlap looks like so that timing works out • Managing dinnertime around activities so that everyone ends up getting fed, especially if different kids/adults have activities that end/start at different times

	• Planning to have snacks and entertainment for those not participating in the activity so they are not bored while waiting for the activity to finish for the participating person • Setting up payments so that all the activities get paid on time so no one gets turned away from an activity • Purchasing any supplies or uniforms so the person can participate • Planning for possible tournaments/ competitions that could happen if team/person makes it that far in a competition activity
Date nights	• Planning time away for just the adults to reconnect • Looking for ideas on places or activities that would be fun • Checking with partner to see if it would be something they would like to do also • Calling and asking questions, if needed • Making reservations, if needed • Coordinating calendars • Note: These can also include family date nights and many of the same steps
Vacations	• Researching websites for fun activities and places to go • Talking to others about their

	experiences and the dos and don'ts of different places • Checking with partner to see whether it is a place they want to try out too • Calling and asking questions, if needed • Researching airlines, road-trip routes, cruise info, rental car info, hotel locations, and prices • Gathering prices for all the things—travel (air, land, sea); rental car, if needed; hotel, if needed; tickets to activities, if needed; gas; food • Discussing budget and seeing whether this trip is feasible • Packing for each person—ensuring that everyone has what they need, making purchases before trip, packing bags with clothes, packing entertainment bag to keep everyone busy on the journey, arranging snacks and food so no one gets hangry • Note: This is similar for both family and couples vacations

Table 1.1: Long-Term Planning

She may have all these long- and short-term plans to keep life moving in a smooth manner. We all know that unexpected things happen, so she has to be able to be flexible and move things around. For example, a child gets invited to a birthday party but forgets to mention it until the day before, causing a huge ripple in the plans—now they have to get a present, wrap it, get the kid to sign a card, and do a drop-off and pickup from the party location. There goes a bunch of time that was probably already earmarked for other things that now must be pushed.

Everything gets prioritized, with some things just having to be done (like feeding the family and going to certain activities). Some are a mid-level priority and get done if everything is going to plan (certain cleaning tasks or her wanting to do something), and others are a low-level priority and get done if there is time and energy for them (these depend on the person but usually involve the activities that are self-care for her and intimacy). Planning is a huge part of her mental load, but it is just that, a *part* of the mental load.

Remembering

Another aspect of the mental load is remembering. There is so much remembering involved throughout the day. This includes not just making the plans but remembering them and all the little details. It also involves remembering everything about each person while carrying out different tasks to ensure everyone's needs are met.

Let's try another exercise and see what happens.

In the space below, write down what is involved in making dinner for your family. Give yourself a few minutes to think about what it takes to make dinner for your family, and write down all the parts involved, including what you think would be the mental load associated with this task.

Exercise 1.2: Mental Load for Making Dinner

Now that you are finished, let's look through the table below for what she is thinking about when making dinner for the family and compare it to what you came up with in your list.

• The parts for the meal • Who likes what • Who won't eat what parts • Who doesn't eat if food is touching • Who can handle what textures • Availability of ingredients • The variety of foods	• Who only eats off what plate/color • Who needs what drink • Who needs to sit where to eat best • Who eats food at what temperature • How to get a conversation going at dinner • Who needs food cut up and how

Table 1.2: Mental Load for Making Dinner

REFLECTION 1.2: Remembering
(Pause here to reflect on your list and on the table.)

What similarities and differences do you notice about your list and hers?

_____

_____

_____

_____

_____

_____

What does this mean to you as you notice the differences?

_____

_____

_____

_____

_____

What understanding are you beginning to develop about her?

_____

_____

_____

_____

_____

_____

_____

Much of the mental load is remembering, and it is remembering for each person in the household, not just for her, which is disproportionate between men and women.[6] Notice how, in her list, the actual cooking of food is only one thing, and there are many more details to making dinner that she is thinking about and then putting into action. Have you ever had a child, or seen a clip on a movie or TV show, say something along the lines of, "Mommy makes it better"? Kids say that line because she is taking on such a large mental load just to make a meal, and men typically are not even aware of all those things.

She is remembering what time things need to happen, where to be, who needs what, where things are, what items are low, and things for each child and even for you. Have you ever asked her where something is and she knew? How about the time for something or what's for dinner or where your keys were and she knew the answer? That is all mental load. That is all her—remembering for everyone in the family.

Delegating

Traditionally, it is common that men do not recognize the mental load on women for domestic issues. As men learn about it and the difference between unpaid and paid labor, they are more willing to help now than even a generation ago; however, they tend to wait to be told what to do instead of owning any of the responsibilities.[7] Women own two-thirds of what it takes to manage life, both the *thinking* work and a

---

6 Ahn et al., 2017.
7 Tuohy, 2022.

lot of the *doing* work.[8] Men are not yet an equal coordinator of the mental load; rather, they are in a transitional helper role that actually adds more mental demand to her, as she needs to determine exactly what requests to make of you, check that it has been followed through with, request again if it has not been, and do it herself if you do not want to complete the request.

Why is it considered helping when you do a task, but when she does a task, it is expected? Have you ever stopped and considered this conundrum? When she has the kids, she is taking care of her children, but when you have the kids, you are watching (some even say *babysitting*) the kids *for* her. When she cleans or cooks, she is simply doing what she should be doing, but when you clean or cook, you are considered such a good partner and *help her* out so much. This unequal expectation is part of why she has to delegate, because society tells her it is all on her to know what needs to be done and let everyone else know what to do and when.[9]

Delegating is one of the hardest tasks of the mental load, as this is the part where she can get accused of being a nag or being too critical. This poem below wonderfully describes exactly how women often feel about having to "nag" to their family.

---

8 Dalgleish, 2023; Tuohy, 2022.
9 Tammelin, 2021.

There was a mom who was called a "nag,"
by her partner, her children, and she swears she once saw the dog roll
his eyes when she was complaining about dog hair on the couch.

And the truth is,
it would be nice if someone thought about—everyone's schedules,
making doctor's appointments,
packing lunches and snacks,
buying gifts for birthdays,
keeping track of what groceries are running low,
everyone's mental well-being,
vacuuming the crumbs off the kitchen floor—
and it didn't all fall on her.

It would be nice if she didn't have to carry the whole family,
and they could carry some of their own weight without her reminding
them ten times.

But, if she doesn't do it herself or delegate,
it won't get done.

And when they finally make the bed or clean up their room,
it needs to be congratulated or applauded,
or they won't do it again.

While for her,
it's expected,
and hardly noticed.

And she's tired of telling everyone what to do,
of praying her partner has the same urgency and level of care she has
when she asks him to perform a task,
of her partner agreeing to do XYZ to "help her out" when it's their
house, too,
of telling everyone to do all the things they should instinctively do,
and being fed up when one of her children or her partner calls her a
"nag."

Because she doesn't want to micromanage,
she just wants to get everything done for the people she loves most:
her family.

—*Danielle Sherman-Lazar | @livingfullaftered*

She truly does not want to be the one to go around reminding everyone of all the things that they need to do. She hates being the person to stop the fun and enforce the tasks that are mundane and must be done for health or responsibility, like bedtime routines or homework. She doesn't like to ask you to do something that may cause a disagreement, because she just wants to be close to you.

What does owning a responsibility mean? It means owning everything about it from the first step to the last, including all the thought processes and the physical work involved. No one tells you what needs to be done for that responsibility; you take care of it. Maybe you have to research something to learn about it, take a class, or talk to a friend who has more experience, but you are the one to take the action to learn.

An example of owning a domestic responsibility that you, as a man, probably already do is yardwork. You think about when to mow, weed, edge, and (over)seed. You consider when to turn on the sprinklers and when to turn them off, as well as what time of year they should come off and on. You make sure they are disconnected in winter so the pipes don't break. You decide whether you mulch or bag your grass, what kind of tools you need that will be most helpful for you, and which purchases to make. You do a lot of thinking work that you then turn into action, and you own the process from beginning to end. Sometimes she may come out and help with parts of it, and you would tell her what to do and how to help, but it is still all your task.

REFLECTION 1.3: Delegating

How did reading the poem affect your thoughts on her delegating?

What do you think about delegating and nagging now?

How had you considered your role of helper before versus now? What tasks do you fully own at home?

What tasks do you think she fully owns at home?

What changes do you think need to be made to be more equitable about owning responsibilities?

Mark is aware that Sandy does a lot of chores at home. He knows that there are certain chores that she expects him to do, too, like taking out the garbage every night. He works all day himself, so he thinks that he will either get to it when he feels like it or, most of the time, he just waits for Sandy to remind him to do it. Unfortunately, he forgets that waiting for Sandy to remind him usually comes at an inconvenient time for him, and then he begrudgingly will get the task accomplished, but he will be frustrated at being interrupted from what he was doing that was more enjoyable, and then Sandy always seems irritated about asking him to do it. Why is that?

When Sandy has to remind Mark to do a chore that he knows he is responsible for, she feels like she does not have an equal partner in the relationship but has an additional child that she is constantly parenting when he is home, and that is not sexy to her. She is frustrated and drained from feeling like she takes care of everything alone instead of with a second adult who is capable and competent. However, the societal pressure of living up to the role as a female—nurturer, caretaker, and homemaker—says Sandy needs to be okay with this responsibility without the assistance of her partner. While this cultural expectation is slowly changing, and men are becoming more willing to help,[10] they are still learning how to be equal partners, so at this moment they are in helper roles as they learn how to build egalitarian relationships. Each relationship can get to an egalitarian level where both partners know how to be equal partners and

---

10 Cherkasskaya & Rosario, 2017.

show up fully in the relationship and home. They can then teach this to the next generation, making it easier for them in their relationships. Societal expectations of egalitarian partnerships will become the norm for future generations.

In this type of relationship, both partners will expect themselves to remember to do tasks that they are supposed to be responsible for without the other to have a responsibility for part of it and then have blame placed on them for not doing their part to remind them, or frustration with them for reminding them at the wrong time. Rather, there is trust that the task will get done and an initiative to actually complete the task, whether they want to or not. In this same scenario, Sandy would not have said anything to Mark about taking out the trash, because she would trust that he will take it out, as it is his task, and Mark would think to himself that he should take it out before he sits down to enjoy himself with something else, as he knows it is not his favorite thing to do.

Reviewing

Finally, women review everything that has been done. This task of the mental load is to ensure all actions have happened as they should and nothing has been forgotten, like a child's homework assignment, doctor visit aftercare, or daily hygiene.[11] During this task, she will review what happened during the day and begin planning any follow-up actions. If something had to be skipped because a higher-priority

---

11 Harrington & Reese-Melancon, 2022.

item came in, like an unexpected birthday party, and some tasks got bumped, then she will start adding them to her lists on future days, because they still need to be completed.

She will usually attempt to talk to her partner about any problems that she has noticed. She will want to go over possible solutions and ideas for how to make things work and, if possible, ask for his help on the tasks that she needs help on, like getting kids to two different locations at the same time or putting something heavy up high. For everything that is talked about during the review with him, though, she will have an expectation on herself to ensure that it is followed through with and completed. At this point she will begin the process over again to begin planning for the next day, now that she has reviewed the day. The mental load is a never-ending process and a constant stream of thought.

REFLECTION 1.4: Reviewing

How much did you know about her reviewing her day?

What did you know about your part in reviewing and her need
for you to help with problem solving?

How does it affect you to know all the parts of mental load
now and how intensive it is?

Putting It All Together

An example of how all the aspects of mental load intertwine with our couple is Sandy planning a day when she has to drop her youngest off at preschool and her oldest off at kindergarten, then go to a doctor's appointment for one child and a sports practice for another. She also has cleaning, meal prepping, and making a grocery run, and in the evening dinner, cleanup, and a bedtime routine (planning) all have to be coordinated so she can pick up and drop off everyone so no one is late and nothing is missed (remembering). She is thinking she may have to ask Mark to help with either cleaning up after dinner or getting kids into their bath (delegation of action) so that she has enough time to get both tasks accomplished before bedtime so she does not have to stay up too late.

Finally, she will review what happened during the day (reviewing how it went) once she gets into bed, so she can see whether she was able to get everything done that needed to be done and move over anything that she couldn't finish and begin planning any follow-up actions needed for anything, or if everything was properly done that day (starting all over again). She will talk to Mark about any problems that she notices so they can agree on a solution, but more than likely she will be the one to follow up on making sure the solution is followed through with. She is hoping he is in a mood to listen to her and that the conversation will go quickly and smoothly so they can move on to other things, as she is tired of thinking.

Chapter 2:

Why Is Mental
Load So Draining?

Since Sandy has children, and this means that she is on call 24/7 and is never truly off the clock at home, even though that job is unpaid. She uses much of her mental capacity and working memory to keep track of what child likes what foods, what dish they will eat off this week, whether they have enough clothing that fits them right now, how much they are eating (and if it is more than normal, does that mean they are getting ready for another growth spurt, and if so, then do they have next-size-up clothes ready to go, or does she need to go shopping?), what kind of stories they enjoy listening to, what time is a good time for bedtime so they are getting enough sleep, how to do bedtime routine so that they are calm and ready for sleep when it is bedtime, how much exercise they are getting during the day, how much screen time they are getting, the best way to discipline—and all of this is just part of the thoughts on the children.

There is also keeping track of when food items are low; making grocery lists; deciding breakfast, lunch, dinner, and snacks for the home; determining what the cleaning schedule should be and what Mark needs her to do; and, finally, identifying what her own needs are to keep herself healthy. Brain energy usually goes in that order, too, a vast amount on the children's needs, a large portion on home management to keep things running, remembering what the spouse's tasks for her were for the day, and, finally, if there is anything left, planning for her own self-care.[12] Mark's mental capacity does not extend much to the kids or home management. He does have to consider tasks for work to keep his business running successfully, but it is within the normal operating functions and not an overuse of his brain system, and even when it is heavily loaded, it is not the same constant weight she bears.

Executive Functioning

What am I talking about here? This is the executive functioning system in the prefrontal cortex of the brain, and maybe you have heard of it before. Let's break it down to get even more clear on what it is and how it plays a part in our everyday lives. The generally accepted definition of executive functioning is the neural processes necessary to regulate emotions, to solve problems, to make deliberate decisions,

---

12 Rutherford et al., 2018; Yatziv et al., 2018.

and to enable effective planning, reflective learning, and working memory.[13] Executive functioning is how humans manage their working memory to successfully learn and manage life,[14] and this is what she is using for the mental load with all the planning memory, delegating, and reviewing.

The prefrontal cortex area is what controls thoughts and behaviors that work together to allow people to make and accomplish goals and regulate themselves.[15] Without executive functioning, people would not be able to regulate their attention, intentionally retrieve information from their long-term memory, engage in all the steps involved in completing tasks, or manage social situations that include people's abilities to solve problems, manage emotions, resolve conflicts, strategize and make plans, and take practical risks.[16] Humans use this brain system every day, which develops slowly in childhood and adolescence and shapes how people deal with many of the challenges that are a part of living. The last thing to take note of about the executive functioning system is that when a person is overwhelmed, it can be hard to manage emotions or feel capable of making deliberate decisions, solving problems, or resolving conflicts.[17] We will delve more into that experience shortly.

Now that you know a little about executive functioning and how we use it to learn, make decisions, solve problems, plan, regulate our emotions, manage our life, and perform all these other extremely important aspects of living daily

---

13 Kalyuga, 2011; Yatziv et al., 2018; Zainal & Newman, 2022.
14 Kalyuga, 2011.
15 Yatziv et al., 2018.
16 Zainal & Newman, 2022.
17 Wilton et al., 2021.

life, how does it affect her with the mental load we were talking about earlier? While executive functioning is used every day to learn, regulate emotions, and complete tasks, it has a limited capacity and can handle only so much input at any time. When it is overloaded, task completion, focus, and even mood can be negatively affected.[18]

Much of the available capability of executive functioning for a woman's main focus is on the needs of her children.[19] This focus is necessary to be able to care for them, as they cannot care for themselves. To stay in this attentional focus, women's brains will inhibit distractions from the child's care and make it hard to focus on her own needs or anything other than what is in the best interest of the child.[20] This attentional focus can make it difficult and create change in the relationship with the adult partners as the focus goes from each other to the child. This doesn't mean she needs you less; she needs you more, and it will just look different now.

When parents have a more secure attachment to each other and are able to consider each other's perspectives more readily, their connection and relationship overall fares better.[21] You can put yourself in each other's shoes and think about how they are doing and even what might help them. Your mind doesn't get stuck thinking only about yourself and your needs but can expand to incorporate your partner's needs, too, and you know that when we are showing up for the other, they are more likely to show up for us too.

---

18 Gamble et al., 2023.
19 Yatziv et al., 2018.
20 Yatziv et al., 2018.
21 Jessee et al., 2018.

While staying attuned to the needs of the child, the mother also has to be able to shift tasks to handle other demands such as cooking, preparing to leave the house, or making appointments, while also managing her own emotions to not upset the emotions of the child.[22] These shifting tasks can be a challenge and are especially hard to manage simultaneously, and they are a part of an overloaded executive functioning system.

That was a lot right there. It is a bit heavy and heady. Before you had kids, her focus was on you. Now that you have kids, her focus has shifted to her children instead of only you. You are not alone. Many men feel this way. It is backed by research that her brain is trained to feel a sense of responsibility, consistent with social norms, that focuses on them to keep the child alive, because human babies cannot keep themselves alive for years, and they rely on their adult providers, usually the mother. They are not independent for many years and need her help and guidance during that time. It isn't because she loves you less or no longer wants you, but because they *need* her and her mind attunes to their needs to the point that even her needs do not get met. While she loves those kids, she probably also misses you and being able to take care of herself.

---

22 Rutherford et al., 2018.

REFLECTION 2.1: Executive Functioning

What did you learn about executive functioning?

What parts of executive functioning have you realized are affecting her heavily?

How does learning that her focusing on the children is biological and not a choice affect you?

How much of the skill building for executive functioning do you think you have done?

What areas of executive functioning skills can you improve on?

Yes, executive functioning is a system that all humans have and use daily. It is their mental capacity and working memory for keeping track of daily life, including their jobs and home management. When you go to work, you manage everything there using your executive functioning skills to keep up on deadlines and tasks so that you can keep your job. Those daily skills are all part of a normal executive functioning operation, and, when used within this capacity, it actually feels good and productive.[23]

Both executive functioning and mental load can use up a lot of the limited mental capacity, which can be mentally exhausting and overwhelming if there is no honest rest to recover each day. Working memory can hold only so much information at any given time each day, and if the focus of attention is on processing information and making decisions, then there will not be any capacity left to let go and be in the present later in the day.

If a lot is going on with the kids, the relationship, new challenges, life schedule, and managing the home, the system may be overloaded for a while. Once that capacity is reached, the person feels drained and overwhelmed, thus affecting their abilities. However, if processing remains within the capacity of working memory, then it actually feels satisfying,[24] meaning that if we can stay in the black, then the day feels good, but if we go into the red and have used more than we have, then the day feels overwhelming and draining.

Mental load is using up space and resources of the

23 Trujillo, 2019.
24 Trujillo, 2019.

executive functioning system as it processes information to make decisions, form plans, and coordinate activities for all persons in the family system. The executive functioning system also underlies prosocial abilities. If the mental load is too high, it can have an inverse effect on social abilities like empathy, compassion, and patience for others because the executive functioning capacity is lowered.[25] This can make it hard to see things from others' perspectives or offer empathy when the brain already feels stretched too thin.

Sandy may have a hard time leaning in to Mark with compassion or patience when she is feeling overloaded from using up all her brain energy, and she does not have any capacity left in her executive functioning system to provide the social abilities to give him what he needs. Have you ever had this happen to you where she seems quiet or unsociable with you and you don't understand why? It may be an outward show of the invisible workload that she has for that day and how much is going on inside her that is affecting her social skills and abilities.

Home managers keep track of themselves, their partners, children, pets, home, plants, and all the things that are needed to keep those things alive, happy, functional, and working. If both adults in the home have a job, home managing typically still falls to one person in the relationship for the majority of the work, resulting in her working around ninety hours of both paid and unpaid labor per week.[26] This entails a lot of mental capacity and working memory, trying to keep up with all the parts of life that need

25 Gamble et al., 2023.
26 Dalgleish, 2023.

attention just to keep life functional at home and at work. Sometimes she works more paid hours than he does each week, and she still does more of the unpaid labor at home. In chapter four we will get to why she always seems to do more of the unpaid labor regardless of whether she has a job. If she keeps going with unpaid labor 24/7, whether or not she also has a paid-labor job, and never gets a break, then mental fatigue can set in (feeling forever tired).

Fatigue That Comes with Mental Load

She is using a lot of cognitive energy throughout the entire day, with the mental load and executive functioning hitting maximum capacity. Yet, even when she is at maximum, she will still keep trying to push through, because it has to get done and she feels she doesn't have anyone else to lean on. When this overexertion happens day in and day out for an extended period, cognitive (a.k.a. mental) fatigue can set in.

The brain has a limited capacity for processing information and making decisions, and when this resource is maxed out, processing information and making decisions becomes automatic rather than intentional. Once that capacity limit has been hit, using an excessive amount generates mental fatigue that affects the person's ability to function well.[27] We talked about how the mental load is within the executive functioning system, and it is accounting for the needs of each person in the household, considering the possibilities for how to meet those needs, making a decision on which possibility to go with, and then reviewing those decisions

---

27 Trujillo, 2019.

to make adjustments as needed.[28] All that brain labor can lend itself to an excessive amount of overuse of that limited energy, leading to mental, decision-making, and emotional fatigue if enough time for healthy recovery is not given each day. Once in that fatigued mental state, the person's ability to complete tasks and make decisions is negatively affected.[29] If she continues to keep going at the same pace, then exhaustion from being mentally overstimulated will set in, and it becomes even harder on her to deal with the mental load she is trying to juggle.

The brain needs time to recharge so that it has capacity the next day to begin anew for another day of functioning. When people use their brain energy to the max each day, they can feel fatigued, which can impair their functioning by the end of the day and make it hard to make decisions or process information. When fatigue is continual, it can turn to exhaustion and start to affect the ability to complete tasks, increase emotional stress, and decrease the ability to regulate and manage self.[30] Unlike fatigue, which sets in at the end of the day because the daily energy has been used up, now there has not been a recovery of the energy, and the person is starting the day with less energy. This exhaustion can lead to mental health issues like psychological distress, anxiety, and depression, along with feelings of dissatisfaction with life.[31] If a person enters exhaustion and does not get help with it, then they could spiral with mental health issues. It is important that they feel supported and can rely on their

28 McLean et al., 2023.
29 Trujillo, 2019; Díaz-García et al., 2022.
30 Balconi et al., 2023.
31 Ciciolla & Luthar, 2019.

partner to understand how they are feeling and that their partner can tolerate their emotional and mental state.[32]

Basically, cognitive fatigue happens when there is too much happening mentally, resulting in a feeling of overall exhaustion and then a lack of ambition to do anything.[33] She is so burned out by running the daily life of everyone that there is no room in her head for thoughts of her own pleasure, self-care, or sexual desires. Mental fatigue can be so encompassing that it affects all areas of the person, including an increase of feeling exhausted, a lower motivation to complete tasks, and an increase in reaction time that stems from high mental load that includes anxiety or stress and an overflowing executive functioning system.[34] It is common to have to think about multiple things during the day, which is why humans have an executive functioning system, including working memory, to help them with processing information that they need daily and what they are using in the moment to complete a task. Normally, use of this system is not an issue and is quite natural; the problem is when it becomes overloaded and there is still more going on without enough time for rest—causing fatigue.

When working at an optimal level, the working memory ignores distractions and remains on task, but when it is reaching overloaded levels, it is harder for it to weed out irrelevant data and is more distracted.[35] Throughout the day, it is quite common for people to take care of multiple tasks and have information also coming at them that would be a

---

32 Jessee et al., 2018.
33 Salomone et al., 2021.
34 Díaz-García et al., 2022.
35 Chen et al., 2021.

nice detour, and when they are able to focus on the necessary information to complete the task, then they do not take the detours but can save them for another time. However, when they are overwhelmed, it can be hard to filter what is a distraction and what is relevant to complete the task at hand, so it becomes easier to get sidetracked and lose focus.[36] You might see this when she gets sidetracked and loses focus on a task to scroll on her phone or start on another task before finishing the task she was in the middle of already.

Another interesting thing about cognitive fatigue is that when people become fatigued, they tend to lose the ability that allows them to engage inhibition and refrain from negative responses toward others.[37] Instead of having patience with Mark, Sandy will get irritated at him more readily and be less likely to regulate her emotions with him when he is unsympathetic or misunderstanding what she needs from him. There are probably times you can think of where she seemed moody or irritable and you couldn't figure out why, as you didn't think you had done anything wrong. Most likely this is a time when she is mentally fatigued and having a hard time regulating her emotions.

One more component of mental fatigue is decision fatigue. Making decisions uses up limited space in the executive functioning system and can affect fatigue when the allocated space is full and a question is asked with a decision expected.[38] Did you know that you can make only so many conscious decisions in a day before experiencing decision

---

36 Minamoto et al., 2015; Föyen et al., 2023.
37 Salomone et al., 2021; Gamble et al., 2023.
38 Trujillo, 2019.

fatigue? So, when someone asks Sandy a simple question and she responds with an answer akin to "I do not know," it is because she has no room left in her head to process even a simple question and calculate a practical answer. It can seem like a simple question, like what movie to watch or where to go for dinner, but it feels impossible to make a decision. This is a moment where it can feel overwhelming and exhausting.

This has probably happened to both of you from time to time, depending on what kind of job you go to each day. We can make only so many effortful decisions in a day, and once those are used up, it is hard to make decisions for the rest of the day. Have you ever had a time where you couldn't decide where to eat for dinner, but when the other person suggested places, you would say no to those places even though you couldn't decide on a place yourself? You had decision fatigue. You knew you wanted something but couldn't quite explain it.

Another way it presents is anytime someone asks you a question, it feels so huge that you cannot process the question, so you respond with an answer that sounds similar to "I don't know." You do not answer that way because you are trying to be difficult; it is because you have run out of mental capacity to make decisions, so that is the only answer that doesn't feel too hard to say. Unfortunately, she makes so many decisions every single day for everything in the home that she experiences decision fatigue almost daily (if not every day).

REFLECTION 2.2: Mental Fatigue

What did you know about mental fatigue before?

_____

_____

_____

_____

_____

What is helpful to know about mental fatigue now?

_____

_____

_____

_____

_____

How does mental fatigue show up in your partner?

_____

_____

_____

_____

_____

When do you see decision fatigue affecting her?

_____

_____

_____

_____

_____

Impact of Constant Mental Load

If we think of attention like a valuable currency that gets reloaded every day, and you only have so much each day to spend,[39] we can see that mental load is an overspending when it is just one person trying to manage it. When women are spending more than they have, they are becoming burned out, exhausted, and overwhelmed with mental fatigue, as previously mentioned. Women also deal with higher rates of mental distress, such as depression and anxiety over the constant worrying from their mental load.[40] Research shows that depression and anxiety are related to an over-used executive functioning system.[41] When women are constantly spending their mental currency on thinking about home management, scheduling, and family needs and are not able to rebuild the currency level so they have more to spend, this can create an overuse that opens them up to vulnerability to anxiety, depression, exhaustion, and mental fatigue. In a way, they are going into mental debt, which taxes the mind to the point of exhaustion, allowing for big consequences like fatigue, depression, and anxiety. Sometimes she will say something that lets you know she is overspending her attention. She might say she is already tired from tomorrow, or she might wake up feeling like she is already at 75 percent, or she might let you know about the anxiety or depression she is feeling.

The mental load affects women daily because the cognitive demands are there 24/7 and she never gets a break from

---

39 Pitts, 2023.
40 Bird, 1999; Schilperoort, 2021; McLean et al., 2023.
41 Zainal & Newman, 2022.

them. Even when going on vacation, she thinks about the things that need to be remembered or done and check in on people who may be taking care of the house, pets, children, or plants to ensure the tasks are being accomplished as necessary. It would be hard to shut this thought train off, because who else will pick up the slack if she were to let go? She needs someone who has proved to her that they will be there in her place so she can shut it off. This 24/7 daily processing includes the big daily task of remembering to do all the things that need to be done and the timing of when to accomplish them so that the household runs smoothly. Women have internalized societal pressure to be the brain of the family regardless of whether they work outside of the home or make more money than their partner.[42] It is expected that she will organize the family, household, and schedules for everyone regardless of whether she is doing that full-time as an unpaid home manager or if she also has a full-time paid career on top of the unpaid home manager job.[43]

If she also works outside of the home, then she carries the mental load of managing the family life on top of the mental load of managing her work life as well and how to incorporate the two, as her workday is the one affected if something happens with a child during working hours.[44] Think about whose phone number is the contact for the school to call in case of emergencies, and even if both numbers are available to the school, think about whom they call first. In most

---

42 Ahn et al., 2017.
43 Shelton & John, 1996; Ciciolla & Luthar, 2019; Çevik & Wright, 2023.
44 Pitts, 2023.

situations, if a child is ill or cannot go to school for whatever reason, it is she who has to make accommodations or stay home with the child. The constant stream of thought from the mental load takes up so much time and space that it can even make it hard for her to enjoy downtime like vacations or even sleep at night.

There have been reported sleep issues and higher evening cortisol levels due to too much mental load.[45] It is hard to relax at home when there is a constant reminder of the never-ending list of things to be completed, so the stress hormone, norepinephrine, remains high in the evening when women do not feel that their partner will take initiative to complete tasks that need to be done equally.[46] When there is a lot of daily stress or too much on the mind, it can affect the body's ability to regulate its sleep-wake cycle, resulting in sleep issues.[47] It becomes harder to fall asleep at night when there are constant worrying thoughts racing around in the mind and keeping a person awake; ironically, less sleep can also increase the stress level and amount of worrying.[48]

Sandy has a constant mental load that she is processing all day long, trying to keep track of and ensure nothing is falling through the cracks in her family, and when it is finally time for sleep, her mind refuses to slow down, making it hard to fall asleep at night. She might look forward to bed all day long and feel tired throughout the day, but when it is finally time, all she can do is stare at the ceiling or lie in the dark with a million thoughts going through her mind

---

45 McLean et al., 2023.
46 Bird, 1999.
47 Kalmbach et al., 2023.
48 Yoo et al., 2023.

of the tasks still to do or the things she needs to remember or may have forgotten. She cannot focus on anything else. Even when she is supposed to be enjoying downtime in the evening or doing something for herself, her mind is still distracted by the never-ending list. This is not healthy rest and unfortunately does not help her to recover and be ready for the next day. Mark does not see this constant thinking and processing in Sandy's mind. He thinks that she is actually enjoying her downtime and getting some peace when it looks like she is resting in the evening or before they go to sleep.

It has been noted that there has been an increase in relational conflict when there is an excessive mental load.[49] There is a feeling of being overwhelmed by more to do than can be done in one day for her, and him not feeling the same pressure to be worried about the needs of the household, lending to relational dissatisfaction.[50] It would be easy for this to lead to relational conflict due to bitterness or resentment on her part for feeling like she is doing everything and then seeing her partner not doing anything because he does not feel that same pressure or have that same list running through his mind. For him it could feel like the upset from her is coming out of left field, as he truly does not understand all the emotional and cognitive work she is going through and how he is not being a supportive partner. Don't worry, we will get to how to be supportive in part three so that you know what to do.

---

49 McLean et al., 2023.
50 Ciciolla & Luthar, 2019.

REFLECTION 2.3: Impacts

What did you not know about how mental load affects her that you know now?

How much mental currency do you use and how much does your wife use?

Do you think you go into mental currency debt every day? Explain.

In what ways can you see the ramifications affecting your wife now?

The problem with mental load and the impact it has on her is that the mental load is invisible, so you only see the consequences it is having on her without seeing the why. If you see someone working on something physically for many hours throughout one day, it makes sense to you that they would be exhausted that night. If you see them do this hard physical labor day in and day out with little rest between shifts, it would make sense to you that it is wearing on them and that they may struggle, be more tired, or suffer other consequences. The difference here is that this exhausting labor is invisible. While the consequences are still just as profound, it is harder for it to make sense to you without being able to see the labor that is involved.

Chapter 3:

What Is the Imbalance of Power Between Men and Women?

This chapter might be challenging for you for a variety of reasons. The theme may be something that you have never considered before, that you have considered but not truly understood, or that you struggle with believing to be true for women. It is okay to be challenged by what you are reading; it is how we grow and become better humans. It might be hard to take in because it isn't your experience or you don't want this imbalance to be there, so you don't do anything to intentionally create it—but it still exists. You might not want to believe it is there because it hurts you that it exists, so you don't want to acknowledge it, or because acknowledging it means you might have to put in effort to do something about it and you don't want to put in that kind of energy. There are many possibilities on why this chapter might be challenging for you to read, and it is okay to recognize it is hard and then stay strong and read it anyway. Face the hard and allow the growth to happen by becoming aware of what you may not be aware of yet.

If it becomes difficult to read this chapter, pause and ask yourself some questions. If you feel frustrated about reading, also pause and ask yourself what you are reading that is bringing up this feeling. Ask yourself if you are ready to change or want to stay in the same headspace you have been stuck in already. Ask yourself if your partner is worth challenging yourself to learn a new way of thinking, even if it is different from how you may have been raised or from the ideals you may have internalized for a long time.

How Does It Start?

From the time that parents find out they are having a daughter during pregnancy, there begins an expectation of what it means to be a girl in their culture.[51] Immediately, adjectives are used to describe her, and colors and themes are picked for a nursery to show how the parents feel a girl should be raised. Female babies are seen to match the gendered expectations for girls, and those social norms typically include soft, weak, sensitive, and fine-featured, which are typically different from when they expect a boy.[52]

Daughters are then raised to be more communal, with expectations for warmth, caring, kindheartedness, and

---

51 Ahn et al., 2017; Hardies, 2022; McConnon et al., 2022.
52 Imhoff & Hoffmann, 2023.

thoughtfulness to others.[53] An expectation to be more communal means that they should think of others' needs before their own. So, right from the beginning, women are shaped to believe that they should be putting others before themselves. In most families, sons do not receive this same type of communal expectation. If daughters do not embrace those expected qualities, they are seen as rebellious or other negative perspectives like bossy, stubborn, or difficult. From birth, there are many messages that are coming toward this little girl, both implicitly and explicitly, that tell her how she should be, talk, behave, and think in all areas of her life. As she grows, she may not even realize this is happening to her, and she may not be able to even pinpoint where the messages came from, just that she knows these things to be true. She doesn't realize it because many of these messages are so subtle that you do not know you are receiving them. She internalizes them and just knows things to be true about how she should be but struggles to describe where she learned that idea.

All these messages over time can have a psychological impact on the female, whether she knows it or not. These messages tell her whether she is good enough and are internalized so that on conscious and unconscious levels women act in ways that they feel society expects of them. Boys also received messages for how to be a man, like maybe you internalized that when you walk through a door, you hold it open for a woman, or you walk on a woman's left side so that you are on the side closest to the street. However, like

---

53 Imhoff & Hoffmann, 2023.

girls, boys may or may not be able to explain when or where they learned those messages. You have an idea of what it is to be manly based on what society and family has taught you, and if that idea were to be challenged, it would become an internal struggle as you either reject it or make room for it.

Society has many gendered expectations for men and women. Women have evolved with society to be expected to be communal because they give birth, raise children, do unpaid domestic labor, and are seen as weaker and more vulnerable to men, so they do not have as much power.[54] Society tends to have the power to regulate its members' behavior that is taken for granted as just how things should be.[55] Most members of their societies don't tend to act outside of their standard group norms, because if they do, there are consequences that feel isolating or rebuffing.

When women act outside of accepted behavioral expectations, they are treated poorly, rejected, and called names by both men and women. Most people do not want to feel these negative consequences, so they stay within acceptable norms. Due to the way society has this regulatory power, change happens slowly, over generations, and we are in the midst of change now for moving toward egalitarian relationships. These gender norms of how she should behave are explicitly and implicitly taught from birth through parenting, church, schools, friends, and the media—magazines, television, movies, commercials, and now social media.[56] Everywhere they go there are messages that tell them how

---

54 Huntsinger & Raoul, 2022.
55 Parfenova & Kozlova, 2023.
56 Johri, 2023.

it is to be feminine, and if they want to fit in, then they need to follow these norms.

Women and men are raised with an idea of what are acceptable roles for adults in society and in relationships. Women have typical roles that are seen as acceptable and even encouraged by society, like having a career but expecting to put that on hold to raise children, or more likely to manage their family and career simultaneously.[57] Many families now need the dual income of both adults working, so she will often work again once she is able, but she will still be the one who manages all the things for the child.

It is her role to be available to the child if the child is sick or there is a holiday at school/childcare, so she will have to arrange alternate childcare or use a sick day to stay home with them, meaning that she is responsible for all the unpaid labor that goes into managing a family and home in addition to her paid-labor time at work.[58] Women are expected to be the nurturers, caretakers, organizers, and the ones whom anyone in the family can go to at any time to help with any issue.

Women are socially taught that they should want to be mothers, and if they do not want that, then there is something wrong with them.[59] Society has deemed that a woman is considered rebellious if she doesn't want to become a mother. Think about when you got married and some of the first questions your wife received were about when she was going to have a baby, how many children she was going to

57 Halie & Harrison, 2021.
58 McConnon et al., 2022.
59 La Rochebrochard & Rozée, 2022.

have, and whether she was going to work or stay home once she had children. Women who choose not to have children suffer consequences from society that can feel isolating, or and they might even be rejected by other women because they are not carrying out a *woman's purpose*. This is an expectation that falls upon women, even though in a marriage there are two people.

REFLECTION 3.1: Expectations

What are some expectations you have about women?

_____

_____

_____

_____

Where did those expectations come from?

_____

_____

_____

_____

If you truly consider those expectations, do they fit for you or do you believe them because it was what you thought you should expect? Explain.

_____

_____

_____

_____

_____

What expectations would be helpful to change?

_____

_____

_____

_____

When Sandy was young, she had a sister and a brother, and she can remember how she and her sister had to do chores every day while her mom and dad worked. They had to clean the kitchen, do the laundry, sweep, clean the bathrooms, and keep their bedroom tidy. Their brother had to take out the garbage from around the house once a week the night before trash day, take out and bring in the trash cans to the curb, mow the grass once a week, keep his belongings out of the common areas, and keep his bedroom tidy. It never seemed fair to Sandy, because her and her sister's chores were daily and took a lot of time, while her brother's chores were not. Most of them were only a few minutes' worth of time, or something like mowing the lawn took about an hour and a half, but it was only once a week. Her and her sister's chores had to be done multiple times per day or had multiple steps to complete and were time consuming. Her mom told her that is just how boys' and girls' chores were and to not complain about it.

So she grew up thinking it didn't seem fair but received the message that you take care of others and do the hard tasks without complaining or expecting a lot of help in return. She learned that if she complained, she would just be reprimanded for not wanting to help her mom out and thinking only of herself instead. She learned that isn't how good girls thought and that good girls wanted to take care of others and show support for their family. She would see her brother and her dad sitting on the couch, enjoying their free time, and internalize that guys get more free time to pursue their interests than girls because girls have to take care of others first before they get time for themselves, and boys don't have to do the same.

As she grew older, she would hang out with other girlfriends, and they all had partners, so when they got together sometimes it would become a conversation about who has to do what, whose partners are not involved at all, and who has managed to get a partner who actually helps, with the unicorn seeming to be a partner who has initiative to do things without being asked. This tells her that there are men out there who can overcome the messaging about gender identity and show up in a way that feels like a whole partner to their spouse. How do they do it?

While the societal expectation is that she has to carry this mental load alone, the *desperate desire* is to have an equal partner who can carry a balanced weight of the mental load so that she does not have such an overloaded mind. The ideal partner is someone who can grasp what she means by initiative with mental load and egalitarian relationship instead of responding with something akin to "I want to help, just tell me what to do." She sighs and feels sad that she must be resigned to how life is and has been since she was a child, and she has no hope that it will ever change. It is disempowering to always be weighed down with everything for the family.

Feelings About Self

With all these expectations of what it is to be female and all the weight to do all the things for everyone, perhaps the most confusing is the pride associated with thinking of everyone else's needs first and her own last. There comes a great deal of shame if she is not able to be exactly what it is that she has internalized as an ideal woman. Shame involves feelings of emotional distress, inferiority, low self-esteem, inadequacy, and a negative affect.[60] Feelings of chronic shame affect health much like chronic stress, as both raise stress hormones that affect feelings of general health in day-to-day life.[61]

Women will also feel shame when they begin to compare themselves to others and see themselves as not doing as well, so they will feel guilty and judged even if there is no evidence to feel that way.[62] She will see herself as not being a good enough wife, mother, or homemaker and compare herself to others without even knowing their full story. Remember how she has internalized this ideal of what a good girl does and this high expectation that she now tries to live up to constantly? Women are constantly battling feelings of shame about everything they do in life based on expectations that are too high instead of being satisfied with the concept of good enough and giving themselves the same grace they tend to typically give to others.

She tends to think that everyone else has everything all figured out and she is the one who doesn't get how to manage this overwhelming mental load. Women try to make it seem like they have it all together for the outside world to see, but inside they feel like they are failing at almost everything. They apologize anytime someone comes over, and asks them to please ignore the mess even if the house isn't that messy

60 McGarity-Shipley et al., 2023.
61 McGarity-Shipley et al., 2023.
62 Wojciechowska, 2023.

or not realizing that it is perfectly acceptable to have messes when you have young children. This internalized societal shame of expecting herself to be a perfect woman adds undue stress to her that makes it only harder to function.

Many times women internalize feelings about themselves negatively as they grow up. All their lives they are surrounded by messages from the media, society, and religion, telling them to be skinnier, prettier, smarter, nicer, more communal, and more virtuous. Often they feel that they are never enough and are falling short of expectations for those around them, which makes it hard to feel good about themselves and gives them a very loud inner critic. This inner critic is constantly telling them about their downfalls and how they screwed up all throughout the day. It doesn't allow them to be okay with being good enough; rather it tells them how what they did could have been better and that they will never be good enough, which lowers their self-esteem.

Self-esteem is how one feels about oneself, and if it is high, then they believe they have value to other people, and it helps them to be adaptive in situations, while on the other side, if it is low, then there tends to be a loss of confidence, high levels of depression, anxiety, poor mood, and less enjoyment of life.[63] It is hard to have good self-esteem when you have this inner critic talking down to you every day. Self-esteem development begins in childhood, and if it is not nurtured in a way that is showing the child they have value, but instead is showing them that they will never quite get it right, then their inner voice develops to also criticize them.

---

63 Holas et al., 2023.

When Sandy was in high school, she struggled with math. She had a test coming up for algebra class, so she studied every day after school and did extra problems to make sure she understood the material for the upcoming test. The day came and she took the exam. When she was given the test score, she had passed with a 99 percent and she was so excited. She was proud of herself for all the hard work she had done and finally received an A on an exam—a high A score, even. She happily showed her father her exam paper that night when he got home from work, expecting him to also be proud of her, and instead he looked at her grade and seriously questioned why, if she had studied so hard, she had not gotten 100 percent instead of *only* 99 percent.

She deflated instantly, and all the joy from her hard work left her. So did the idea that good enough was acceptable. In its place was the idea that perfection was all that mattered. *To truly be considered good enough, you must be perfect.* From that day forward, she never let up on herself, and her inner critic was very hard on her. She demanded perfection from herself, and if she didn't perform to her exacting standards, then she put herself down and had no self-compassion.

Self-compassion is how a person cares about themself, and they show this through how they are kind versus self-critical, through community versus isolation, and through mindfulness versus their inner critic. When a person is high in self-compassion, they can give themself warmth during hard times, whereas if they have low self-compassion, they will feel critical of themselves and as though the pain they are experiencing is deserved.[64]

Many times women can give compassion to others easily, but to themselves it is practically unthinkable. This happens because of stories like Sandy's, where she internalizes extremely high expectations early in life, and these carry with her into adulthood. It becomes even harder to be self-compassionate if that message is reinforced often from family, friends, and partners. She will believe that everyone else is doing better than her, and even if they struggle, too, it is for a good reason, whereas she is just not good enough or a failure. Imagine striving for perfection while never being convinced you will achieve it. If a woman does not have high self-esteem or self-compassion, then her sense of worth, confidence, and even how she prioritizes herself in life will all be affected negatively.

---

64 Holas et al., 2023.

REFLECTION 3.2: Feelings About Self

How much did you know about self-esteem and shame being tied together?

How do you view good enough versus perfection?

Do you think she expects perfection from herself with many tasks?

How much compassion do you think she has for herself?

How do you think you could help build some compassion within?

How do you think her self-esteem and self-compassion plays into her mood and general feelings around the home?

Societal Norms That Create an Imbalance

The perceptions involved in the previously talked-about traditional roles tend to leave an imbalance of power between males and females. For example, in relationships where the male has control over the finances, there is a propensity for a large power imbalance.[65] They tend to have a relationship where she has to ask for money to spend anything, yet she is still expected to buy necessities like groceries and clothing for growing children. Due to not having access to the family money yet needing to ask for money weekly to buy the necessities puts her in a position of having to constantly ask for money or even defend why she once again needs more money to be able to care for the family even though he knows very well why she needs money. Retaining control over family money and restricting access in this way have more to do with controlling her and feeling powerful than it does with helping someone who may struggle with poor spending habits.

There are other ways to manage finances that do not promote this kind of imbalance of power and even financial abuse. If you find yourself in a situation where this is how you are handling the family money, take a moment to ask yourself why you want to manage it in this way and what other ways it could be managed that do not require her to come to you to ask permission so often. Try other methods out until you find one that feels good to both of you, because we are going for equality.

Women tend to also do more of the household

---

65 Tammelin, 2021.

management, even when they both have careers, and even if she makes more money, and this is likely due to the socialization they receive growing up, which leads them to believe it is their responsibility for the unpaid work at home.[66]

Maybe you are wondering how this is a power imbalance. *I will help out at home. I have chores I take care of too.* Most of the time men do not have Groundhog Day chores; they have limited-time-only chores. So this is a power imbalance, because the woman can work 24/7, but the man can clock out and then only have to do those things at home that society says are a man's work, like yardwork or grilling, for example, which are not Groundhog Day chores like laundry and cleaning the kitchen. He will end up with time to do what he wants because he has finished his limited-time-only chores, and she will always have something that needs to be done, so she ends up with very little time to do what she wants or will feel guilty for taking that time.[67] There always being something that needs to be done is why it is so hard for women to just rest at home. They then have to make a deliberate choice to ignore the task that needs to be accomplished and try to do the restful thing they want to do instead. Anxiety or that inner critic will sneak in and start giving her a hard time about resting when there is so much to do that it is hard to enjoy the rest.

Society has expectations of what is normal for each gender, and this in itself creates a power imbalance because social norms expect the man to be above the woman in the areas that create influence or power, like finances, politics,

66 Ahn et al., 2017; McConnon et al., 2022.
67 Tammelin, 2021.

and influential careers. If the woman is higher than the man in those areas, then she is considered unorthodox and given negative labels.[68] This can be seen by the double standards in how women and men are judged when a woman is a boss versus when a man is a boss, or when a woman is out with her children versus when a man is.[69]

Women can do the same things a man would when they are in a position of power, but because they are women, they are looked down upon, belittled, and insulted when the man doing the same things would be respected, listened to, and appreciated. You can see it every day just by noticing at work, in politics, on the news, or anywhere that there could be positions of power and a woman might get into a bigger role than secretary. Once you are aware of it and know what to look for, you will notice it, but until you know, you just don't recognize it happening around you.

Even though women are just as capable as men, our society was developed to not want women to be men's equals but to be their followers. This ideal has been changing over the past few generations, but some of the societal norms are having a hard time catching up to the new ways of thinking. This is why society promotes privilege only if a person is masculine-male with a male-dominated and male-centered structure that oppresses and exploits women or feminine-males.[70]

The research indicates that many of the power imbalances start with social and gender norms that are internalized

68 Hardies, 2022.
69 La Rochebrochard & Rozée, 2022.
70 Johri, 2023.

growing up and perpetuated each generation. So, even though changes are happening and more people are okay with women being in positions of power, working toward egalitarian relationships, sharing the unpaid labor equally, and not gendering household tasks, there is still a group that believes women should not be equal to men and should stay subservient to them. This is scary, as it perpetuates possible threats to women.

**REFLECTION 3.3: Societal Norms That
Create an Imbalance**

What norms had you not known about that create an imbalance of power?

How are you feeling about imbalances of power as you read this chapter?

What came up for you as you considered why it might be hard for her to truly rest at home?

In what ways do you think control happens in the relationship that you hadn't ever considered before?

How do you notice women being judged more harshly than men for the same actions?

Possible Threats

Women face possible threats to their physical person and emotional safety just for being a woman. That is not to say every man out there (including you) is against women or wants to hurt them if given the opportunity. Rather, I am suggesting that there is a general negative reaction when women step outside of what has been designated their roles for how to behave, work, dress, caretake, and talk. So, when women enter into anything typically considered a male role, such as a CEO in a company, a political figurehead, or something competitive, they are typically seen with hostile sexism and devalued in that role, unlike their male counterparts, simply because it does not fit the lens of how women should be seen, which is as communal caretakers, not competitive leaders.[71] Again, now that you are aware this happens, think about times it has happened or take notice when a woman is in an influential position that would typically be reserved for men and take in how she is treated. Ask yourself, If she were a man, what would the responses be then?

Research shows that societies that promote traditional gender roles also encourage social norms for dominating women, abusing women, and viewing women as lesser.[72] Our society has encouraged those social norms, as our history is filled with laws where husbands were allowed to beat their wives. Women had rules to control them, such as not being able to open their own checking accounts, and there were rules about what women could wear in public. Some of those rules existed as recently as during our grandparents'

---

71 Diekman et al., 2004.
72 Gangal et al., 2024.

lives. Some believe those laws and rules should not have been changed and that women should still be under the full control of men. These are scary thoughts for many women, to know that there are those out there who would want to control and even hurt them simply because they are female. So women have to worry about whether they will be hurt by their partner, someone on the street, or someone in the workplace, not because they did anything wrong, but because they were a disempowered gender in the eyes of certain men. This can make it hard to know whom to trust.

Women are taught to not walk alone at night, or to be defensive by carrying keys between their fingers or keeping pepper spray in their purses. They are taught not to dress in certain ways because they may be asking for sexual violence to come their way. These teachings are unique to their gender, as men do not have to learn these things or even consider them. In this same way, women are taught implicitly that their role is to be communal and that they do not have the power to be above men, but instead they should smile, be accommodating, and follow the norms, as this is self-protection against possible threats from men.[73] She learns that it is her job to think about what might set a man off, that he is not responsible for controlling his own emotions or urges. Society teaches women that if a man hurts her, then she did something to cause him to do it, because if she had not been so drunk, worn such short or tight clothing, or acted so enticing, then he would not have raped, assaulted, or harmed her. It is her responsibility to

---

73 Huntsinger & Raoul, 2022.

know how all men will react to her and be prepared to either behave properly so they do not get out of control or be able to protect herself so no harm comes to her if he were to act out. It seems like the message from society is that men are more powerful because they are bigger, they are stronger, and they can choose not to harm a woman, and women are to be aware of the potential for danger at all times.

Sandy was making a quick run to the grocery store to pick up a few items for dinner that night before she had to pick up the kids from their respective schools. As she parked her car, she was grabbing her purse and made eye contact in the side mirror of a man in a car a couple of rows up. The man was parked next to the entrance to the store. She froze. She wouldn't be able to get inside without going by this guy's car, and he seemed suspicious.

After they made eye contact, he put his head down. What was he doing? What should she do? It would probably be fine and nothing would happen. Other scenarios raced through her mind: What if he grabbed her as she was walking past and pushed her into his car? What if he was a serial killer? A rapist? A rapist serial killer? What if he wanted to harass her and give her a hard time? Maybe he would get out and follow her around the store because it made him feel good to scare women, and then he would pretend like he was just shopping when she freaked out.

Ugh, what should she do, just skip this dinner plan and do something else instead? She could make the kids happy and get takeout tonight. After a couple of minutes, he still had his head down. *What was he doing?* she wondered. *Maybe I will just play it safe and leave. This is weird, and I just don't feel safe right now.* Suddenly the guy lifted his head and put his car in reverse. He slowly drove out of the parking lot, and she watched him to make sure he fully exited the parking lot and drove off. Then, before going inside to do her quick shopping, she waited another minute to make sure he didn't do a U-turn and come back.

While this guy didn't do anything to Sandy other than make eye contact for a couple of seconds, it set off alarm bells in her head, and she went on high alert to keep herself safe. If Mark had been with her, she would have been fine and not thought anything of it, but when she is alone, she is constantly thinking about keeping herself safe in public settings.

REFLECTION 3.4: Possible Threats

What consideration have you ever given to what daily threats are out there for women?

What did you know about how women are taught to protect themselves from unknown men?

Can you think of times where you have thought of women as lesser even if you didn't act on it?

What might be changing about how you think of women as you process more about thinking of them on an equal level?

What might be something you are struggling with right now as you process the threats women face?

What would it be like for you to constantly be thinking about threats around you while you are just trying to live your life?

I know this may have been a hard chapter to read, but you made it through. Some emotions may have come up for you, and you may have wanted to stop reading. Thank you for staying and doing the hard thing to challenge your thoughts. Maybe nothing changed for you, and maybe you gained some insight into experiences you never knew were happening for her. These are experiences of women, and that doesn't mean that you want them to happen, but it also doesn't negate the fact that she has to live with the fact that other men do, and she has to be careful.

Chapter 4

What Are the Gender Expectations?

Social Norms for Men and Women: History of Unequal Unpaid Labors

Why is it different for men and women with unpaid domestic responsibilities? Where does this idea come from for men that it is their partner's responsibility to do most of the unpaid labor around the home? Why does he consider it "helping" her out, but it isn't helping him out when she does the same things? These might be questions you have never thought about before. It isn't until we become aware of something that we can process why we believe something without question. We can process it together here so that you have more of an answer than "because" or "that's how it's always been" and, instead, you have an understanding that might help you want to make changes for your relationship.

As explained earlier, from birth women and men are raised with different expectations by society and their parents. She internalizes these expectations to develop an idea of what is and is not acceptable for men's and women's behaviors. Society does not have the same expectations for men and women, and if women do not go along with what is considered acceptable, then they risk being ostracized or bullied for being different.

Society is going through a revamp of what it means to be a man or a woman, and some in older generations are fighting against what those in younger generations are reconstructing to be considered acceptable. Currently, it is all about breaking chains and generational curses to enhance and better the lives of those living life *now* instead of doing something just because it has always been done but not because you truly believe it is how it should be done.[74] Questions are being asked about why we do things, and younger generations do not tolerate answers of "because" or anything similar; in fact, if the answer does not make sense, then they are challenging it. You see this with parenting and how parents have moved away from corporal punishment and toward the newer parenting style called Gentle (a.k.a. authoritative) Parenting, which includes talking with the child in a way that makes them feel safe without yelling or hitting them. In this book we are talking about the mental load of the unpaid domestic labor that traditionally women have done. But the question we address in this chapter is, Why is it that women have responsibility for the domestic work and not men?

---

74 Bünning, 2020.

Remember, when boys and girls are young, they typically have different chores. There are some chores that are considered to be for boys and some that are considered to be for girls. Think about those chores right now and what you would be asked to do compared to what a girl would be asked to do. What are those chores that come to the top of your mind? Things like mowing the lawn, taking out the garbage, helping Dad/Mom clean the garage, yard work, and maybe cleaning up your bedroom. Now, what were the chores that the girls were asked to do? They would be chores like cleaning the kitchen, vacuuming, laundry, mopping, dusting, and cooking. What is the difference between these chores?

The chores that the girls are doing are tasks that are never completed. The kitchen gets messy again the second someone puts a dish in the sink or makes themself something to eat or begins to make dinner, so the joy of it being clean is short-lived. Laundry is never fully complete, as people are wearing clothes, so even if she manages to get everything washed, dried, folded, and put away, there will be dirty clothes in the baskets again that evening, so that joy of having it all completed is again short-lived. It is mostly similar with vacuuming, mopping, dusting, and cooking—as soon as someone steps on the floor it is dirty again, dust is constantly floating around and landing on stuff, and humans need to eat every few hours. These are Groundhog Day chores: regularly repeating. Whereas the chores that the boys are asked to do are not. They are chores that are able to be completed: the limited-time-only chores. Take the garbage out once every couple of days and once it is done it is complete until the next time it is full. Yard work has to be done once per week and once it is done, it is done for days until the next time it has to be completed. Big tasks like helping clean out a garage or attic are once- or twice-per-year tasks that once complete are done until the next time they need to be tackled.

The tasks that have to be thought about constantly every day and multiple times per day are the tasks that are given to girls who then grow up to have this mental load where they think about even more things constantly and expand it to thinking about all the things for everyone in the family. The tasks that are thought about sporadically are the ones that are given to boys, so they do not develop the skill of thinking about things constantly. It is not that men cannot do it; it is that they did not get the same amount of practice growing up. When boys get more practice, they grow up to be able to carry a mental load easier and more naturally. You can develop this skill now, even if you did not practice it when you were younger. It is within you, just as it was within her.

REFLECTION 4.1: Unpaid Labor History

What kind of chores did you have when you were a youth?

How much practice did you get with developing mental load skills as a youth?

What consideration did you ever give to the difference between Groundhog Day chores and limited-time-only chores?

How many Groundhog Day chores do you take complete responsibility for now?

How many Groundhog Day chores does your partner take complete responsibility for now?

Media Messaging

When you look at TV shows and movies, what are the jobs that women are portrayed doing historically? They show her being a housewife and taking care of her home, children, and husband: Think of any old black-and-white show like *I Love Lucy* or *The Andy Griffith Show*, and many other shows like *Rules of Engagement* or *That '70s Show*. If she has a job, she is shown still being a great housewife and managing all the things while also rocking her job and being amazing there, too, like in any doctor show. The message is that she can do both and be fully satisfied without needing help or being overwhelmed. Sometimes the message is that it can get overwhelming at first, but once she figures it out, then it will all seem easy, and she will be able to handle it.

I will let you in on a secret: That is all fantasy and definitely not rooted in reality. When they show a woman who is in a high-power job, they usually show her as an awful person who doesn't care about other people. These are all the societal messages that women grow up internalizing, and they are reinforced to both men and women through the media.

So, when a woman begins thinking about what kind of life she wants to have as an adult and she wants to be seen as a good person, she will gravitate toward being a communal or family-oriented person, because it is ingrained in her that those women are the ones who are good people. Even if they have a job, they should be taking care of their family. They don't want to be the woman who comes across as awful in the high-power job, because nobody likes her, and she is always seen as the villain.

Then there is written media like magazines and books. Magazines aimed at women are all about how to keep a better house, organize better, take care of family better, raise kids, decorate, follow recipes, clean, and cook. Again, the messaging that comes across is that if you want to be a good woman, then you need to take care of others. You should be able to clean, cook, take care of your family's needs, look good for your partner, and keep a pretty home. More recently, you can find articles in some magazines about self-care, but that has been a newer trend. The internalized message again is that if she wants to be a good woman, then her focus needs to be on her family and doing all the things, which is a lot to hold in her mind.

Until very recently, there has not been a message that it is okay to ask for help. Instead, it has been that you should do everything on your own and make it seem like you are happy to do it. Even when she cries about how hard or overwhelmed she is, many times she hides to do it. Only in the past couple of years has the mental load been truly named and have there been conversations about it. You can find many conversations on all the social media platforms about mental load, and there are even some great guys coaching men in how to understand it and take it on more in the relationship to become more egalitarian. I will include them in the resource section at the end of this book so you can follow them if you would like for your continued learning.

There have been books written about it for her to understand what is going on and books for both to help the couple have conversation around it, with the language to actually talk about it. Previous to that it was hard to even describe, because there wasn't a name for it, and neither person knew what was going on for her, except that sometimes she struggled.

REFLECTION 4.2: Media Messaging

How had you thought about the media influencing your idea of what it is to be a woman?

Have you ever been aware that women in powerful roles in the media are portrayed as bad/mean?

What kinds of things did you think were in written media for women?

What do you think about the messaging that the media sends to women and how it matches our societal expectations for women?

In what ways do you want to see the media change its messaging in the future?

Part 2:

How Does Mental Load Affect Her Desire for Sex?

Chapter 5:

How Is This a Relational Problem?

This Is Not a <u>HER</u> Problem; It Is a <u>WE</u> Problem

In the past, when there were issues with sex in the relationship, she would go to therapy alone to work through "her" issues. It was seen as a problem within her that the couple wasn't having *enough* sex. She was the problem, and if she would just go and figure herself out, then all would be well. There was this idea that she had psychological blocks to having sex, or her sexual desire needed to be adjusted to match his, and then all would be well. Unfortunately, this just wasn't true, and it has been found that sexual issues in a relationship are a relational issue, not an individual one.

There is not a magic pill that fixes all sexual issues, even if there are medications that can aid in some sexual dysfunctions. Instead, working on the relationship and sexual experiences together, with the aid of medications, if necessary, produces longer-lasting effects.[75] Sometimes, when we are sexually frustrated, we say things that push us further apart from each other, when in all honesty we are desperate to get closer to the other person. When partners feel emotionally connected to each other, then sexual activity tends to be higher than for those who do not feel close.[76] This probably makes a lot of sense to you, because it is easier to have desire for each other when we are feeling emotionally connected, so of course sexual activity tends to be higher for couples who are more emotionally connected. When we are low in that connectedness, then trying to be intimate can feel awkward or tense, so it doesn't happen often or isn't very enjoyable when it does happen, and then we feel stuck in a negative sexual cycle. So it makes sense that the couple would be having the problem and not just one person, and fixing the relationship would be more effective than attempting to fix the person. When partners work on the problem together, they can hear what each is struggling with around the issue, and they can then be responsive to each other's unmet needs, which has shown to lead to higher sexual and relational satisfaction.[77] Sometimes they are stuck and need a couples sex therapist to guide them through the stickiness so they can come out the other side, but if both are willing to do the work, then it can be done.

Together the couple can work to rebuild their emotional approachability and responsiveness so they feel a secure

75 Johnson & Zuccarini, 2010.
76 Træen & Kvalem, 2023.
77 Vowels et al., 2022.

sense of attachment with each other, which allows for space to have intimacy and sexual pleasure, because they feel emotionally safe with each other.[78] You will want to develop your sexual voices so you can find playfulness in intimacy and sex instead of it being a checkbox item, thus stimulating attraction and trust in the experience. This will guide you to find your relational and sexual styles, including balancing meeting your and your partner's sexual needs so it feels safe and pleasurable.[79] These goals would be tricky to meet without both people present in the work and doing their part to recover and get out of the negative sexual cycle you find yourselves stuck in. It isn't about simply increasing the amount of sexual interactions, but increasing the connection you have so that you feel intimately connected, which can lead to sexual experiences that don't feel forced.

There is more to intimacy than just sex. The emotional connection between the couple matters just as much and can influence how the couple's satisfaction around sexual experiences rises or falls.[80] There is communal strength in recognizing each other's needs and meeting them in a relationship, and this is there for communal sex as well. When a couple has strong communal sex, they are able to engage in sexual activities for the purpose of increasing intimacy and making their partner happy, which increases relational and sexual satisfaction.[81] This communal strength is also beneficial to the relationship when one person notices and is responsive to times that sex is not of interest to a partner.

---

78 Johnson & Zuccarini, 2010.
79 Girard, 2019.
80 Walker & Lutmer, 2023.
81 Hogue et al., 2019.

If they are understanding of this need to find another way to connect intimately, relational and sexual satisfaction can remain high.[82]

To encourage high communal sexual strength, the couple needs to talk about and discover the sexual needs that are necessary to both of them, alone or with the guidance of a therapist. Through this process, they can foster intimacy and sexual experiences that are stable within those standards so both feel their needs will be met without an overfocus on meeting only one person's needs.[83] The couple can talk and find the ways that build emotional, intimate connection between them so they feel closer together, constructing an easy pathway toward sexual desire that does not feel forced or performative for either.

High communal strength shows up in that both partners are satisfied. If both partners are giving a little ground, then they are getting some of what they need and giving up some, too, which means that each is getting around 50 percent of their desires, which is more equitable than one getting all and the other getting none. Having high communal strength will build a resiliency in the relationship, and partners will know the other is thinking about their needs, too, and it isn't all about one person getting fulfillment, but that *both* are important in this relationship.

---

82 Muise, 2017.
83 Impett et al., 2015.

REFLECTION 5.1: It's a We Problem

If you reflect on your initial thoughts, did you think this was a her problem or a we one?

How much had you considered you both had parts to work on to reconnect intimately?

What kind of emotional accessibility and responsiveness do you think you provide to her?

What does playfulness around sex and intimacy look like for your relationship?

What is your communal strength right now?

How can you improve your communal strength so that it feels like you both are getting your needs met?

In what ways do you show her that her needs are important and you want to fulfill them?

Gender Differences About Sex

Have you ever considered the different ways that girls and boys are taught about sex? You see jokes about it in the media—on TV and in movies or if you watch comedy shows. But have you ever actually sat down and thought about the different messaging that girls and boys receive about sex? Did you assume it was similar? Do you think it should be different? If you do, why? What is it that makes it so that women and men who engage in the same act together should think and feel so differently about it? When you see in the media parents getting all fired up about something happening to a daughter, but thinking it is okay or even being proud when it happens to a son, what do you think? Where does this idea come from that sex is good for males but bad for females, when the act takes both sexes?

Males and females are brought up differently and led to believe opposing ideas about sex, even in the same household, because of societal expectations for girls and boys. Males are expected to enjoy sex and have many partners, and women the opposite.[84] While growing up, boys are expected to experiment with sex, look at "dirty" magazines, talk about sex with their male friends, and even to have sexual encounters so they know what they are doing before they get serious with their eventual life partner. If a teenage boy comes home and tells his dad that he had sex, many times his dad does not get angry with him but is proud of him and checks that he used protection. You can see this in the way that TV and movies portray these kinds of scenes. The dad

---

84 Walker & Lutmer, 2023.

will oftentimes, later in a bar scene, proudly tell his friends about how his son had sex, and they will all congratulate him and then reminisce about their teenage sexual experiences.

This is not the same experience for girls. They are expected to remain virgins and be innocent until they are married. They are taught that boys are only after sex, and once they give it to them, they will leave her and she will be alone again. You can see this message portrayed in movies and TV shows also. If a girl comes home and tells her mom that she had sex, most of the time the mom gets upset and tells the father. The dad wants to kill the boy, and the mom is worried about her virtue and possible pregnancy. There is a fear that she will be seen as a slut/tramp/whore because it is not socially acceptable that a woman may enjoy sex, and those who do are deviant women. Which is a mixed message that women try to sort through and can struggle to figure out and we will cover more about in chapter seven.

The societal rules for men and women are paradoxical. The rule for boys involves women, which requires her to break her rule, and if no woman would break the societal rule for women, then men could not meet the societal rule for them. Yet women who will break the rule for females are then called names and seen as deviants, and the men are applauded for their *conquests*. It truly is confusing and leaves women in a bind. How can women do anything right by following either of these societal rules? It is like they are set up to fail from the beginning and then made to feel bad about failing, as though they actually had a choice in the matter when either way seems to cause trouble, depending on whom you talk to.

As partnered adults, women can feel so desexualized with mothering and caregiving that they do not have any parts of themselves left to be sexy or desire sex, as they have nothing left to give, especially if their spouse is more like a dependent than like a partner and has left all the domestic responsibility to her.[85] What does that mean to be more like a dependent than a partner? Kids come up to or yell across the home to her all day long: *Mom . . . Mom . . . Mom . . . I can't find . . . Do you know where? . . . I need . . . Help me with . . . What time? . . . Make me . . .* and on and on. She is running around and answering their questions, thinking through things to figure out what needs to be done, finding things, and looking up answers for times so she can be the source of information. If you think about it, which one describes you more—the way the kids ask questions all day or the way she figures out the answers to the questions all day? Most men, whether they want to admit it or not, fall in the kid-question category. Oftentimes, they joke that she just knows all the answers or it's right there in her head, so it is easier to ask her than to search for it themselves. It makes a lot of sense why they ask her and turn to her for the answers. Unfortunately, it puts them in the dependent category, and it is not sexy. If you want to add some sexiness to yourself in her eyes, instead of asking her the questions, take the time to find the answers for yourself. Then, when you talk to her, you can say something along the lines of, "I wasn't sure what time practice was, so I looked it up on the calendar and saw it's at six p.m., so would you like me to make dinner before

---

85 Harris et al., 2022.

or after practice?" She will definitely see you as more of a partner instead of a dependent.

Women can feel so desexualized with mothering and caregiving that there doesn't feel like there is anything left for sexual desire. Most women have responsive desire, and most men have spontaneous desire. This means that most men get the urge to have sex and are ready to go, whereas most women have to get going before they feel the desire for sex. Helping her feel that intimate connection will help that responsive desire grow, which is why she wants to do romantic things with you before sex. Intimate connection is important if one of you has a responsive desire. You can also ask her what it is that gets that butterfly feeling in her stomach and do some of those activities before sex or have her do one or two if they are individual activities. They could be activities like reading novels with sexy scenes in them, watching movies with sexy scenes in them, giving massages (however it is that *she* likes them), deep talking, flirting, bantering playfully, playing a game, playing sexy games, and role-playing. If you ask with an open mind because you truly want to know so you can make sexual encounters more enjoyable for her, then this could be a great exercise that can be incredible for both of you, and it could help her to feel sexy again.

There is also an unequal intimate emotional burden that females carry where they are processing their desires, feelings, needs, and stimulation as well as those of their male partner. Similarly, she interprets what actions need to be taken and whose needs should be prioritized, all the while processing their mental and emotional capacity to either say something or keep silent about it.[86] *Phew.* That was tiring just to think about doing all that processing. . . . And that is all happening during sex? Did you get all that information, because it was a mouthful? Basically, to break it down into smaller chunks, there is a sexual mental load that women are carrying also for both themselves and for you. She is processing what she is desiring, what she is feeling, what she is needing, and how she is being stimulated in the moment. At the same time, she is processing this for you to the best of her ability by using your body language, tone, sounds, and what she knows about you to ensure you are satisfied before attending to herself. Then she interprets for both you and her what actions need to be taken, including whose needs should be prioritized, while also processing her capacity for whether she should say something or just keep going and stay quiet. Men benefit from this intimate emotional burden and do not typically reciprocate it. High emotional burden lends itself to burnout, sexual and relationship dissatisfaction, and exhaustion, because she will deny her own needs over being others-focused, which men do not do.[87] Women often feel an unreciprocated burden to care for their partners' needs above their own, and this feels unfair and tiresome and can result in what appears to be lower sexual desire, because they just do not have the mental energy to do this sexual mental load that night, so they will find a way to reject a sexual experience.

---

86 Anderson, 2023.
87 Fahs & Swank, 2017.

REFLECTION 5.2: Gender Differences About Sex

In what ways did you ever think about the different ways boys and girls were raised to view sex?

What hit you this time as you really sat and thought about how boys and girls were taught about sex?

What do you think about the paradoxical messaging that is sent to girls about sex and how it seems to be a no-win situation?

In what ways can you be more like a partner than a dependent now that you know how unsexy it is to come across as a dependent?

What did you learn about responsive and spontaneous desire, and how does it help you?

What did you know about all the things she thinks about during a sexual experience?

How does that affect you?

Being Able to Share Likes and Dislikes

So how do we get this to start feeling reciprocated so she doesn't feel like she is carrying this sexual mental load all on her own? Well, we have to start having conversations. I mean the real, deep, open, and honest conversations that are sometimes scary and hard to have because we have to be vulnerable. What if she doesn't get what you are trying to say, laughs at you, or becomes upset? These are all valid worries and are reasonable reasons why it would be scary to have these real conversations. I am not saying it is going to be easy; I am saying that it is important.

Communication is a key component to a relationship, and it is just as important an element when talking about sex as it is about day-to-day living. Perceived partner responsiveness is seeing a partner as caring about your needs, understanding what you are saying, and validating what you can do and your opinions.[88] What does it mean to have perceived partner responsiveness? This means that she has to have the *perspective* that you are caring about her needs, understanding what she is saying, validating her, and showing her that she is important to you. It is essential that she feels like she matters, not that it is all about sex to you and that is the reason you do the things you do.

One way of communicating is with your body language or behaviors. For example, do you barely show affection all week or have minimal conversation, but on the weekend, when you might get sex, suddenly you are very affectionate and super snuggly or kissy? The message that you send in this

---

88 Hogue et al., 2019; Vowels et al., 2022.

case is that you only show up emotionally for your partner when it means you have a higher chance to get sex. Then you might find her tense up or push you away somehow when you give a hug, kiss, or snuggle unexpectedly, because she only expects these behaviors from you when you are saying you want sex, not as a way you message that you enjoy being around her or love her.

She may struggle to tell you what that means because it isn't inherently wrong that you do those behaviors, or even that you want to have sex. It is that you seem to show up *affectionately* only to get sex, and that can make her feel used or manipulated, which doesn't feel good or sexy. When a partner is seen and felt to be responsive, then it is easier to talk about topics that may be challenging, like sex. Having a higher sense of responsiveness about sharing results in higher sexual desire and more sexual and relational satisfaction.[89] If she could share with you and feels that you would be responsive to her need for you to be affectionate at times when it will not lead to sex, and that it is just as okay as the times where it does lead to sex, then it would make her feel better and actually more sexy and loved.

To keep relational and sexual satisfaction high, it is important that when partners share with each other, they do *not* make sex into a quid pro quo situation, where they are keeping track of who did what and when, as this will greatly lower satisfaction overall for both partners.[90] No one likes to feel as though there is a tally board being kept about them, especially when it comes to sexual experiences.

---

89 Vowels et al., 2022.
90 Raposo et al., 2020.

How embarrassing. Neither of you would enjoy that kind of sex life, as it would probably feel like preparing for a battle instead of an intimate encounter each time. We also do not want to use absolutist language when we talk with each other—these words include *never, always,* and *constantly.* These words set us up to not be able to feel heard or to hear each other, which pushes us apart instead of allowing us space to get closer together.

We need to remember that no one gets it wrong all the time, and while we may wish it happened more often, it shouldn't negate that it does happen sometimes. If we can appreciate out loud when something does happen that we like so our partner knows we like it, then it is more likely that it will happen again.

When we are sharing likes and dislikes, it is a vulnerable time. It is important to do because if we do not share with each other, then how is our partner supposed to know if we like or do not like something? No one is a mind reader, unfortunately, so we have to have these sometimes-tricky conversations. We go gently with each other, have an open mind, and remind each other that we are on the same side. You are gaining valuable information that can improve your intimacy and sex life if you are willing to take it in without getting defensive, but instead because you want to meet each other's needs. It is vital that couples be able to share what they do and do not like about sexual encounters, and even more essential is that they feel that their partner hears them, validates it, and is responsive about what is shared.

Mark and Sandy are sitting on the couch after the boys have gone to bed. Mark is scrolling on his phone, and Sandy is reading a book. Sandy puts her book down and looks at Mark with a cautious smile.

SANDY: Mark, I want to try something different but I am afraid to talk to you about it.

MARK: What do you mean try something different? Different about what?

SANDY: I mean about something intimate.

MARK: Oh, what do you want to try?

SANDY: Well, I am afraid to talk to you about it because you always just want to get to the sex part and never want to do the stuff I am interested in doing. *I am afraid to talk to him about this because I don't think he really cares about my needs.*

MARK: What do you mean? I do what you want to do. You just never want to do the sex part, which is what I like doing. *She doesn't care about my needs.*

SANDY: Sure you do it, but you rush through so that you can check the box so we can get to the part you want to do. It doesn't make me feel like you actually care about what I want to do. I feel used. *Why am I trying to talk to him about this? He is already not listening to me.* Never mind. Forget I said anything.

MARK: *Okay, slow down, man, listen to what she is saying. It is about her, not you, right now.* No, I'm sorry. I want to hear what you have to say. I care about you and your needs are important to me. I am sorry that it seems like I rush through what you like to check a box, and I will work on slowing down so you have time to enjoy it, because that is important too. Thank you for sharing that with me. What else did you want to share with me?

SANDY: Wow, thank you for saying that to me. It means a lot, and I feel like you actually heard me. I'm sorry I said "always" and "never," because that's not true. Sometimes you do, and when you do, those are the times that I enjoy myself the most. I need you to slow down more often and take care of my needs first before getting to the part you like, because once you finish, then I usually don't get to, and then there is nothing in it for me. That is a lot of why I am not really interested in sex. It's not about me; it's about you.

MARK: Oh, hmm, I hadn't thought about that before. Why didn't you ever tell me this? I am not a mind reader.

SANDY: I don't know. I just kinda thought you would get it. Isn't it obvious that's why I wouldn't be as interested in sex as often?

MARK: It is not obvious at all. This is really important information. Now that I know this, I can make a really big change. You come first is the new rule.

SANDY: (Laughing.) Wow, I hadn't realized I could talk to you about something like this before or that it would matter so much.

MARK: Anyway . . . what about what you wanted to try . . . ?

SANDY: Oh . . . yeah . . . I wanted to try something . . .

REFLECTION 5.3: Sharing Likes and Dislikes

How often do you and your partner share likes and dislikes with each other?

_____

_____

_____

_____

How does it usually feel when you try to share with each other?

_____

_____

_____

_____

How willing are you to take in what she is saying to you and respond positively to it?

_____

_____

_____

_____

Do you ever notice your defenses going up when she tells you something she doesn't like?

_____

_____

_____

_____

What kind of messages are you sending by your behavior, even if unintentionally, about possibly using affection only as a precursor to sex?

Have you two ever got trapped in quid pro quo or absolutist language patterns? Explain.

What can you do to make sure it feels safe to share likes and dislikes from now on?

Responding to Expressed Needs and Desires for Each Partner Is Essential

Being able to share likes and dislikes is only one part of having good communication between couples, and once a need or desire has been shared to the partner, they then must be motivated and willing to *meet* the need. This is called *communal strength*, and it is vital because couples that are high in communal strength typically see each other as very responsive, which increases sexual and relational satisfaction and sexual desire overall.[91] It increases satisfaction because both people are looking to meet each other's needs, so they are coming more to the middle with expectations. Neither is expecting to get 100 percent their way all the time, because that would mean their partner is not getting what they need, and they do not see that as a fair and respectable way to live in a relationship. Instead, they find it valid that each gets some of their needs met, and they expect that some will not be also.

The caution with having high communal strength is to be careful that it does not become extreme to the point that the focus is so much on the other partner's needs to the detriment of their own and becomes neglectful of what they desire, leaving them unfulfilled in sexual experiences, as this will result in lower sexual desire and sexual and relational dissatisfaction.[92] This care for the other's needs and desires to the neglect of their own is called *unmitigated sexual communion* and will have the opposite effect of communal

---

91 Vowels et al., 2022.
92 Hogue et al., 2019.

strength.[93] The goal is to be meeting closer to the middle of each person's needs so that there is more equity instead of either person getting close to 100 percent of their needs met, as this will build resentment even if the person thinks they want to do that for their partner. It isn't sustainable in the long run, and eventually dissatisfaction will surface.

Interestingly, when a couple has high communal strength and their sexual desires are different, it is easier to have sex, even if one may not be feeling desirous, but still feel satisfaction afterward about the experience and the relationship. Sometimes one may not be feeling it but will want to have sex or be affectionate because it makes the other happy, which in return makes them happy, yet research shows this only seems to work in relationships where the communal strength is high, and it might be because there is trust that if the situation were reversed, they know it would happen for them too. In contrast, those low in communal strength felt low satisfaction when they had sex even when not feeling desirous, showing that high communal strength can be a protective factor for the relationship.[94] Over time, developing a trust in the relationship that each person will be there for the other's needs and desires builds protection for the partnership, making it easier to be there for the other and keeping high relational and sexual satisfaction.

When you talk and share with each other about a need that is there for one in the relationship, the next step is to take what you hear and do something behaviorally with that information. It is hard to be vulnerable, and if you do not

93 Vowels et al., 2022.
94 Impett et al., 2015.

see any changes come from sharing, then it makes it even more challenging to want to share again another time. Ask questions to clarify what you are hearing and what would feel good to show you so you can feel it. This is all about wanting more connection, not to push you away. Work on showing up in the way that was asked and then check in to see if it is going how she was expecting or how you could tweak it some more. This check-in is going to send a message to her that she is important, that you are trying to do what she asked, and that you care if you are getting her. Yes, it is work, but a good, healthy relationship requires work.

Chapter 6:

What Are Sexual Power Imbalances?

Just like chapter three, this chapter could be a bit of a challenge for you. It could challenge your thought process or have you think about things you never thought about before. As with chapter three, that is okay. This is how we grow, gain empathy, and become better people. In this chapter, you will learn things about sex and females that no one may have ever shared with you before or that you have heard but didn't fully appreciate as true. Go slowly with it, read it, and try to take it in with an open heart and mind, as these experiences are probably very different from your own. Again, this doesn't make you a bad person. We are expanding your awareness and knowledge so that you can now use it to be a better partner. Take your time to think through and process the reflection questions, have conversations with your partner to get her individual experiences, and ask questions to get clarity on how you can show up differently if you are ready to do so. You've got this, and we are walking through this together.

Consent

How a person feels about being able to say yes or no to sex and being able to withdraw consent if they change their mind is an important aspect of whether there is equal power or a power imbalance in a relationship. When it comes to sexual satisfaction in a relationship, if a person is having sex not because they want to but because they are trying to avoid negative outcomes, like letting their partner down or trying to avoid a fight, then there will be lower sexual satisfaction for both partners, leading to lower relational satisfaction, and the opposite can also be true: If the person is having sex because they want to express their love, then there is higher sexual and relational satisfaction.[95] There is a difference between just saying yes to give a partner what they want and an enthusiastic yes, showing that she truly does consent to sexual intercourse.[96] Many times she says yes, not because she wants sex, but because she doesn't want to risk the *withdrawal of affection* consequence that can come from saying no. Sometimes this consequence is conscious, but many times it is unconscious. He doesn't realize how much he is hurting her when he pulls away, turns his back, or leaves the room when she says no to sex that night. This withdrawal of affection reinforces her internalized message

95 Muise, 2017.
96 Fahs et al., 2020.

that she is only cared about as long as he is getting sex, that she is a sex object and not actually important as the person she is, and that she is used for sex.

All her life she has grown up with confusing and mixed messages about sex. Once in a committed relationship, it is expected that she will give him sex as a way to keep him from straying, to be a good and dutiful partner, as a way to get children, and to keep him happy. The messaging does not include her pleasure. Nowhere is she told she should enjoy sex; it actually comes out more as a job to do. She is told that when she is in a committed relationship, preferably marriage, that to be a good girl, she should have sex with him, for him, but again nowhere in the message is that she should enjoy it. The part that was messaged to her all her life was that it was acceptable to want affection, and she actually craves affection, because it makes her feel safe, warm, secure, loved, and cared for in a way that sex does not completely fulfill. So when he withdraws affection because she says no to sex, it hurts and sometimes it is a risk she is not willing to take, as she needs the affection more than saying no.

Does it feel safe to say no to sex in your relationship without repercussions? When you ask this question to couples, many times you get answers where he says yes and she says no, which shocks him most of the time. They didn't know there was a power imbalance where he, without having to even think about it, can say no if he isn't in the mood, but that she (1) cannot say no outright and (2) has to do mental gymnastics to figure out how to stay safe while deciding how to say no just the right way or saying yes even though she doesn't mean it.

The reasoning behind the no can vary and entail different traumas or stories that have built to give her cause to believe that she can't say no to sex. It is not usually because she does not feel safe physically. That is not the most common answer I hear as a therapist. It is because she does not feel safe emotionally. There have been times that have happened over and over to tell her that if she says no, she will be penalized emotionally for that no. The question when he asks for sex then becomes, for her, not whether she wants sex, but whether she can handle the consequence of a no or deal with a yes even if she doesn't truly want to say yes.

Yes/No/Okay Without Context Exercise

You can gain a lot of insight from each other by trying out this exercise. It uses only three words and you take turns. One person will start by saying "yes," and the other person will respond with a "no." You go back and forth—three or four times, saying "yes," responding with "no," until the yes person says "okay." The okay must be said without withdrawing affection, so it cannot be said frustratingly, or manipulatively, or in a "whatever" tone. It can be said in a neutral tone, or the best is a warm tone, if the person can manage it. There is no context for this exercise, but you may be surprised to learn how hard it is for one of you to say "no" to the other or to say "okay" without withdrawing affection. If it is this hard to say "no" or "okay" without context, then it can really open your eyes to how hard it can be for one or both of you when it comes to "no" or "okay" when there is context.

This can be a great conversation starter for understanding why you get stuck in negative patterns. It can become a place to be vulnerable with each other and to gain insight into yourself. Go into this with an open heart and mind, as it may seem simple, but many couples have found deep enlightenment and empathy about each other from this exercise. You may also find that you need help with getting unstuck, and it may be time to find a sex or couples therapist to help you.

Exercise 6.1 Yes/No/Okay Without Context Exercise

Women are socialized to believe that their desires are not as important as men's and that they need to make their bodies available to men, affecting their ability to even learn to decipher whether they want sex for themselves when they are in long-term relationships.[97] It can be hard for a woman to give an enthusiastic yes to sex when the power imbalance is so strong against her that not giving consent hints at threats to body, rape, withdrawal of affection, or the relationship unraveling. So she either says an unenthusiastic yes or instead of directly saying no, she offers a soft refusal, like having a headache, not feeling well, or being tired, so that he does not feel outright rejected.[98] If a woman does not even feel okay with saying no to sex, she would not be comfortable to withdraw consent once giving it, even if she did change her mind about it being okay to have sex. There is an imbalance of power between the sexes over feeling like it is okay to say yes or no to sex and what the possible repercussions would be to saying no to a partner.

Where did she ever get the chance to learn what it is that she likes about sex, what she wants, or even what feels good to her body when it has always been about his pleasure first? It's almost like society has set couples up to have a sexual-desire discrepancy and then blamed it on her. You two could work together on discovering her pleasure, though, and make sex something that brings enjoyment to both of you so that it doesn't feel like a checklist item. Get society out of your bedroom so it is just the two of you, and it can be a lot more fun.

---

97 Fahs et al., 2020.
98 Fahs et al., 2020.

REFLECTION 6.1: Consent

How comfortable do you think your partner feels about saying no to you when you want sex? Why?

In what ways do you notice that you withdraw affection from her now that you are aware of it?

In what ways does it affect you to learn how deeply it hurts her and how she can end up feeling used, like she's only a sex object, even though that isn't what you want?

What did you learn about how women are raised with mixed messages about sex?

How does that affect you and your understanding of your partner?

Have you ever asked her whether she feels safe to say no to sex and what she thinks the repercussions are in your relationship? What do you think they are for you two?

How can you work on not penalizing her emotionally if she isn't in the mood for sex?

Orgasm Gap

Desire for women is more about intimacy, emotional connection, and feeling sexually desirable, whereas for men it is about sexual release, orgasm, and pleasuring the other person.[99] Women will fake an orgasm to keep their partner satisfied or because the faux orgasm for her increases his sexual satisfaction, but not because they get anything out of it sexually.[100] When a woman fakes an orgasm, it is because she knows it brings him pleasure, because sometimes it can help him to orgasm, and because she cares about his enjoyment. Even though she doesn't get anything out of the act, it can make her happy to know that she brought him pleasure.

Statistically, there is a gap between men and women in a relationship, with men having consistently more orgasms than women, and over time women may feel disempowered to ask for or take action to achieve orgasm, so they will alter their expectations for what satisfying sex looks like to them, like it not being painful or energy draining.[101] Very rarely does a woman achieve orgasm through penetration. So while it can feel good, it's not going to be like the movies make it seem and you both will achieve orgasm at the same time. That actually almost never happens. Instead, the part of her that has the pleasure sensors is on the outside of her vagina, along her vulva on the clitoris. Playing with this sensitive area can lead to arousal and possibly an orgasm (although there is a small percentage of women who can never achieve orgasm but can still be aroused and enjoy pleasure). You can

99 Sævik & Konijnenberg, 2023.
100 Fahs et al., 2020.
101 Wetzel et al., 2022.

ask her how touching her there will bring about the most pleasure and have some fun experimenting. For most couples, you have to take care of each other one at a time for orgasm; it doesn't happen jointly. If you take an interest in her pleasure and let her feel safe that you are responsive to her sexual needs and enjoyment, too, then she may start to feel empowered to share with you what she wants, which will only increase the satisfaction for both of you.

Even though both men and women have shared that orgasm makes for great sex, the orgasm gap remains as sexual sessions tend to end after the male orgasms, whether or not the female has also orgasmed, causing an imbalance in ensuring that both partners are equally satisfied before the session ends.[102] Why doesn't her satisfaction matter as much as his? She usually takes longer and needs more stimulation to achieve an orgasm from fingers or tongue along that clitoral section of the vulva. It rarely will be achieved through penetration, so if you are done with sex after you orgasm, then focus on her pleasure first and help her find her release before you move on to penetration for yours. Show her that her pleasure is just as important to you as your own through action. For sexual satisfaction, being able to have an orgasm was higher on the list than other variables of sexual functioning.[103] While intimacy and emotional connection are highly valuable markers for getting in the mood and desiring sex, being able to orgasm also makes sex pleasurable and increases the desire to do it again. However, it isn't the only thing there is to make sex enjoyable.

---

102 Walker & Lutmer, 2023.
103 Dienberg et al., 2023.

REFLECTION 6.2: Orgasm Gap

What did you know about the orgasm gap before?

What do you understand about the orgasm gap now?

What did you learn about female orgasms that you didn't know about before?

What difference does this knowledge make for how you will approach sex now?

Expanding the Definition of Sex

When we think about sex, there is a certain idea that comes to the mind about what it entails. Typically, for most people, sex means penetration leading to male orgasm. When that happens, then sex is over, as was just talked about in the previous section. This definition has been the norm, which is communicated everywhere. If you think about movies, television shows, and music, there are some romantic activities that might happen in the evening, and then once they get going in the bedroom, it is a flurry of activity that ends as soon as he orgasms. The media makes this seem hot and exciting, and maybe it is to young men. It leads to issues with consent and orgasm gaps, though, over time. There is also a problem for aged couples if the definition of sex is so narrow as to only include penetration leading to male orgasm. As men get older, sometimes they cannot always hold an erection, so if this is the only definition they know for sex, then they may believe they can no longer have sex when they reach elderly ages. If we can expand the definition to include more than penetration leading to male orgasm, then you can be well into your eighties and nineties and still enjoy a great sex life, if you are healthy.

What does it mean when I say "expanding the definition of sex"? Well, penetration leading to male orgasm is actually only one activity for a sexual encounter, and while it is just fine, there are other activities that could be added to your sexual menu. Sometimes thinking about having sex can have a certain pressure associated with it because you feel like you have to get it up, in, and then ejaculate. We can remove some of the pressure by naming your intimate time something other than sex, like "sexy time," for example. Now, during sexy time, the purpose is to follow the pleasure, and there is no goal for orgasm. Sometimes that will happen for you, for her, or for both, but it isn't the goal. The goal is to follow what feels pleasurable in that moment.

Following the pleasure may seem odd at first, and most men do find it a strange thought process, so you are not alone. Especially since the goal has always been penetration and orgasm for as long as you have been having sex. I am not saying we are taking away penetration or orgasm for you or for her. This actually still happens during sexy time while we are following the pleasure. I am saying we are just not making them be the goal anymore. We are taking away the pressure that we have to get to that goal so that you are not focused on it anymore, and instead your focus is on following where the pleasure might be going that day in that experience.

Now you say you want to go have some sexy time, and she knows that includes her pleasure, too, and she will be more inclined to want to participate. There is no time frame for this either. If you have twenty minutes, then you can go play for that long, or if you have as long as you want, then it ends when one of you says you are done. I have heard sexy times go from twenty minutes to an hour-and-a-half-long experience, depending on what the couple has going on and how much time they have. Sexy time can include communicating the direction of what you want, exploring each other's sensual places, trying out new toys, role-playing, and anything else that you two can think of that brings pleasure to each other. Sometimes it might be following one person's pleasure more than the other, and sometimes it is following both. It builds trust that you value each other's pleasure equally, and it isn't all about one or the other. So when one says they really need something, like penetrative orgasm, it is more readily given, as the other knows their needs will be met also. Sexy time builds sexual communal strength.

Sexy Time: Follow-the-Pleasure Ideas

- Tracing bodies with fingers
- Massaging touch around bodies
- Playing with fingers in hair
- Gazing into each other's eyes while holding hands
- Looking at resource websites together
- Exploring bodies with tongues
- Role-playing—as light or as big as you want
- Body painting
- Being the guide—telling the other what you want, being specific
- Adding in food play—chocolate sauce, whipped cream, ice cubes, etc. (experiment here)
- Taking baths together—bathtub, outdoor kiddie pool, etc.
- Using sex toys—whatever looks fun (experiment here)
- Playing games—find them on websites, sex stores, etc.
- Using subscription boxes
- Making out—kissing passionately
- Kissing everywhere—all over the body
- Trying anything you can think of . . .

The ideas in this list are just that, ideas. You can take what you want and leave what you don't want to use. There are plenty of other ideas that you can look up or come up with on your own. Have a conversation with your partner about what interests her to see what should be included in your list. The purpose of sexy time is to follow what brings pleasure to the body for each of you and enjoy traveling down that road together without an agenda. This is different from the purpose of sex, which has a specific goal, and once that goal is reached, the trip is over. I have worked with couples who have not had sex in years or many months and now enjoy sexy time two to four times per week, sometimes even a couple of times in a day. The reason is that it truly does focus on both people's pleasure and not just on that end goal, where only one person is getting what they need. If sex has been expanded to include everything that brings about sexual/intimate pleasure, then you are both going to be able to enjoy sex well into your eighties.

REFLECTION 6.3: Expanding the Definition of Sex

Have you ever considered your definition of sex before? How?

In what ways can expanding your definition of sex help you and your partner?

How might it be a challenge for you?

What do you think about the idea of sexy time instead of sex?

What would it be like to follow the pleasure for you and for her and get rid of the sex goal?

What follow-the-pleasure ideas would you want to include on your sexy-time menu?

What do you think your partner will think about this idea?

Chapter 7:

What Is Societal Pressure?

Conflicting Messages About Sex

Back in part one of this book, we talked about how confusing the messages can be for women about sex in our society. It can feel like being told two conflicting messages with no right response. If she wants and enjoys sex, she is called a whore or slut, and if she doesn't, then she is a prude. For anything that she does when it comes to sex, society has a derogatory word for it, making it difficult to know what is acceptable and even "right" when it comes to sex for her. It almost seems like she is supposed to want and hate it at the same time, but how does that work?

While being raised, females are presented with explicit and implicit expectations about what it is to be female and how they should present themselves to others and even to themself. These expectations can include the roles she should play, power that others can have over her, the threats of harm that can come to her, and how she should mitigate those like we talked about earlier. There are also psychological, biological, and other feelings around self that affect what it is to be female in our society. She gets bombarded with messages every day through media, as sex is in magazines, in advertisements, in books, on television, in movies, on the radio, and in pictures, as well as from family and friends when they do or do not talk about sex. She will be told in one message that she should be having sex at only certain times or in certain types of relationships and then told to come across as sexy in other messages, so that he will want her. She will be told how shameful it is to enjoy sex or discover what her body enjoys, yet also be told how she needs to have sex with him to keep him, and if she doesn't, then it is her fault if he were to stray or leave her. Family may never talk to her about sex, leaving her to figure it out using only media as a guide, or family may talk about it, which can come with varying messages in itself—some helpful and some harmful, depending on the family.

She is always being told how it isn't men's responsibility to own their behaviors when it comes to sex or lust, that if she acted correctly or dressed properly, then he wouldn't do anything she didn't want. This has more to do with sexual violence or rape, but it is also a message that she is receiving all her life—that it is her responsibility, not men's, to make sure men do not hurt her. This is true for inside or outside of a relationship.

This message typically starts in school, where dress codes are lengthy for the girls but not for the boys. It continues in the news when people blame rape victims and make it their fault instead of blaming the rapist. These are just a couple of examples of how girls are told they have to be responsible for men's actions instead of men. This message can be very confusing and even frustrating for women, as they have to keep their guard up and be careful around all men, since they have been taught that men are not accountable for their actions. Yet she wants to feel safe and loved around a man and be able to trust him to hold himself responsible so they can have a long-term relationship.

In school, as a teenager, the message is typically to just say no to sex. There isn't any talk about discovering your body or what brings her pleasure—no welcoming messages that it is okay to have desires and to find out what it is that she enjoys or to experiment through masturbation so that she knows what feels good to her. Instead, she will be told not to have sex on one hand, and then on the other everyone will be talking about sex creating a sense of pressure to both have and not have sex at the same time. If she were to have sex for the first time, it is very rarely focused on her pleasure and exploring what she enjoys during the sexual experience. Instead, the focus is on penile penetration and male orgasm. This also tends to be a message that gets internalized about sex, that it isn't so much about her pleasure but his. Sometimes this message can be strong and leave her feeling used, like he doesn't really care about her but only about what her body can do for him, or like she is just a sex doll.

What does all this do for her with regard to thinking about sex? It leaves her with unclear ideas about how she should feel about sex and internalizations that tend to war against each other. She may have desires and wants when it comes to sex, but it doesn't feel as though these are allowed to be expressed, so she bottles it up or pushes them away. It can feel like she is supposed to want to have sex only for his pleasure, which over time isn't fulfilling to her. Hopefully you are able to see that there can be many layers to sexual desire and the discrepancy that sometimes happens in relationships.

Sexual desire is defined as interest in sexual activity that brings a person to initiate or enthusiastically consent to receive their partner's initiation of sexual activity.[104] In long-term relationships there are natural ebbs and flows to each person's sexual desires, which can be defined as *sexual-desire discrepancy* when they do not match each other.[105] Sexual-desire discrepancy occurs for many reasons including the inability to schedule time to be alone together, medical problems, hormone levels being off, stress, or relational issues to name a few.[106] Now you have more of an understanding of the different layers that can be involved and where the discrepancies can come from, including that they can even stem from early-childhood messaging. It isn't always as simple as you doing something wrong that is the only impact on her sexual desire. There can be so much more to it that needs to be unpacked or even untangled. While it may feel like it is just something you did that needs to be corrected or that you feel like you can never do it right, if you take into account the additional layers of messages that have been

104 Sutherland et al., 2015.
105 Vowels & Mark, 2020.
106 Mark, 2014.

coming her way from society, family, friends, school, and media since she was a little girl, you are probably only one piece to a very complicated puzzle. Being a safe haven for her to explore and become aware of messages she may not even be aware are affecting her to the degree they are will provide a level of safety for her to figure out what it is that she wants versus what it is that has been forced upon her to accept. Sometimes these sexual-desire discrepancies do not last very long, and other times they last long enough to affect relationship satisfaction.

There are relational reasons that can also challenge the desire discrepancy—for example, finding time to be alone together. After couples introduce children to their relationship, there can be a transitional period while they figure out a new balance between children's time and adults' time. Sometimes children's needs or adult anxieties are so high that it can be more challenging to find alone time between the adults without the children to allow for reconnection. This lack of connection time can affect the ability to feel intimate with each other, even though he usually still wants sex. It is hard to want sex when she is not feeling an emotional or intimate connection to you already, though. Then it brings up those other layers that we were going over at the beginning of this chapter.

Stress, hormone imbalances, or medical issues can all also contribute to a desire discrepancy between the couple. Her stress can go back to the mental load we were talking about in part one, which is huge and encumbering. Hormone imbalances and medical issues are sometimes more subtle issues that, unfortunately, we do not always know about but which can affect her sex drive. Medications that are taken for all types of ailments, including depression or anxiety, can lower her sex drive, and many people are unaware of those side effects in both men and women. Hormones can play a part in not having a desire for sex and then suddenly having an urge for sex as a flood of hormones hit her. This can happen monthly and sometimes become expected as you learn when the hormone wave will hit her, and she may have an increase in sexual desire for a night or two. This is also why as adults get older, sex drives tend to go down in both men and women as hormone balances change.

REFLECTION 7.1: Conflicting Messages

How have you perceived the messages about sex for women growing up?

How does it affect you to consider the confusing messages she has been receiving all her life?

What would it be like to be told you should hate sex but do it to make your partner happy?

What were the messages that you received about sex growing up?

In what ways might that be affecting your relationship?

Have you ever considered that women were told they are responsible for men's actions? How does that sit with you?

What's it like to learn that she may never have been encouraged to explore what brings her pleasure when it comes to sex?

Did you realize there could be so many layers to sexual-desire discrepancy? Explain.

How do you want to make changes to your sexual relationship?

Struggles with Not Feeling Enough

Have you ever felt that the way you do something or who you are just isn't enough for your partner? Sometimes it can be hard to explain to another person, especially your partner, as you care so much about how she feels about you that when you feel like you aren't enough, it can be even harder to bring it up and share that vulnerability. What if she were to agree with you, or what if she hadn't been thinking that way, but now that you bring it up, she gets to thinking about it and starts to think that way now? Feeling like you are not enough can be a terrible feeling, and when it seems like you have behaviors or messages from your partner that back up that feeling, it can be even worse and harder to deny. Many times she can feel this way about intimacy and sex due to societal messages and sometimes even from accidental messages from you. Let's talk about how this can happen, because awareness is the first step in being able to work on something that we may not even know needs to be worked on.

Long-term relationships tend to have less sex in them than there was during the *limerence* phase.[107] The limerence phase of a relationship is the first six months to one year. It is the intense flood of emotions when you want to spend all your time with each other and are finding out all about each other. It is that time of the relationship when you are obsessed with each other. The limerence phase helps us attach to each other and is not meant to last forever, as it burns a lot of energy and uses a lot of time due to the

---

107 Klusmann, 2002.

obsession part of it. As the couple attaches, the phase is supposed to calm down, and the couple is able to get into a rhythm for the relationship that continues the attachment and love without the need for the intense obsession and flood of emotions that take up all your thoughts and energy. This is part of why long-term relationships tend to have less sex in them, and that also has to do with humans needing less sex as they get older. It is completely normal and healthy to not have sex every day, or even every other day in long-term relationships.

Women struggle with gender issues such as body image, feelings around self, and psychological and biological factors. They struggle with feeling confident with themselves, including their body and self-worth, and to believe that they deserve to have their wants and needs attended to just as much as his needs and wants.[108] A lot of this lack of confidence has to do with those conflicting messages from society that makes it difficult to believe that her wants and needs are just as important as yours. Just as we have been talking about throughout this part, not feeling enough is another layer added to the struggle with sexual desire.

The lack of confidence around her body image and feelings about herself can negatively affect her desire for sex. This psychological process to check on her appearance and be overly concerned about her body shape during sexual encounters can have a huge impact on her desire to engage in sexual acts.[109] She is worried about how she looks before having sex, wondering whether she is sexy or pretty enough

---

108 Cherkasskaya & Rosario, 2017.
109 Cherkasskaya & Rosario, 2017.

to you. If she is a mom, she can feel desexualized, because being a mom is not sexy. If you do not feel sexy all day long, and actually feel desexualized, then it can be quite the challenge to switch into a mindset of feeling like you are sexy in the evening, when you might have some alone time with your spouse. So she may try to get into the mindset but is actually then consumed with worry that she isn't sexy, because she hasn't felt it all day.

As women age and after they have children, their bodies can and will change. For many women, this is off-putting, and they struggle with how their body looks now versus how it looked when they were younger or before children. If he is insensitive and teases or makes jokes about her body changes, even if he believes they are playful, they actually can make it worse and cause a lot of pain that can make her even more self-conscious about her body. Remember, she has grown up with unrealistic messages from the media about what an ideal body looks like, and even though we know now that those bodies are airbrushed, starved, or have different genetics, it is still a comparison that gets made about how she is not good enough. She wants to feel good enough for you, and sometimes when she looks in the mirror, she feels disappointment.

Women are also dealing with issues that are biological, such as hormones, menstruation, and instincts to care for children. After women have children, they tend to desire sex less, as they are now caring for the life of another person and that takes priority biologically.[110] It also brings in all

---

110 Klusmann, 2002.

the mental load struggles that we talked about in part one of this book after children enter the relationship. Biological issues like hormones, menstruation, and instincts to care for children can lower sexual desire without the person even being aware of them. Hormones and menstruation can go hand in hand, as hormones can fluctuate during a woman's cycle, which usually is twenty-eight days long. The bleeding portion is the only part that you can actually see, but there is more going on within the body throughout the entire twenty-eight-day cycle.

Hormones can go up and down during this time, which is why I previously mentioned that sometimes you might notice that she has a higher desire at certain times during this cycle (one or two nights), and then other times her hormones might fluctuate in a way that lowers her desire also. Instincts to care for children can be so subtle, yet strong, that she may not realize she has put the intimate part of the relationship on a lower priority, as the care for a child becomes a top priority because that child cannot take care of itself. This is why women are biologically made to focus on the child to ensure its survival. She can struggle with not feeling like a good enough mother or a failure at everything in life if it seems like she is not balancing motherhood and being a spouse well. Sometimes, this feeling can be hidden by defensiveness or anger, as she doesn't want to admit to this vulnerability.

You showing up as a safe place to share by offering empathy and compassion helps with this worry and vulnerability, as you are messaging to her that you want to know, you can be there for her, and you will not brush aside her feelings.

This message is important in her feeling safe to open up to you, which then allows for more emotional connection between the two of you, which is essential in her building a desire for sex.

Sandy feels all these gender burdens on top of all the cognitive weight of executive planning demands, but it is hard for her to explain these additional stressors and fatigue to Mark. It does not feel like he would understand them, and sometimes she is not sure she would be able to explain them to him, as she can feel them but cannot put words to them. Mark is mostly unaware that any of these things are affecting Sandy and of her not being in the mood most nights, so he is unable to have any empathy or provide support to her about it. So many of the things that Sandy is struggling with are in her mind, and if she doesn't share with him, then he is unaware that they are present and affecting their relationship negatively.

On the flip side, if Mark does not seem emotionally approachable and isn't showing that he can stay with her in her emotions, then it can be scary to share something so vulnerable, especially when she is wrestling with how to put the feelings into words. Instead, Sandy shuts down and doesn't say anything and ends up suffering in silence, which feels very lonely, and Mark is left not understanding the deeper roots and only seeing the surface, which lends itself to a feeling of being undesired and unwanted in the relationship.

Sandy tries to test the ability of Mark to be there for her by making comments about herself or a half joke about herself, something small that hints at the vulnerability but easily leaves an escape route if it doesn't seem to go well. She is craving for Mark to respond with empathy or validation about what she says so that she can trust saying more to him. When he teases her about something that happened instead, she shuts down and uses her escape route to steer the conversation away from her vulnerability, while inside she is sad that she can't fully open up to him. Mark has no idea that she wants more from him and thinks that his comment is playful, without realizing she needs something different from him. When it seems like she gets quiet and doesn't have much to say, he is confused and doesn't understand why their playful conversation changed.

Sometimes couples need a therapist's help to get these conversations started and to build the trust and strengthen attachment for responses in the therapy room so that it feels easier to try it at home. Sometimes a couple can read a book, listen to a podcast, or talk to someone and learn a new way to interact or information that gives them an understanding of what might be happening so they can try a different approach. The important part is that something has to happen differently, because if the same methods are tried over and over, they probably are not going to get a different outcome. Introducing a new move in this pattern would change the normal outcome, and sometimes it is trial and error to find the move that makes the most positive change in the relationship. When couples have these positive changes, then they learn how to lean in to each other with more vulnerability so they can support each other and trust that they are there for each other and not going to let them fall.

REFLECTION 7.2: Struggles with Not Feeling Enough

What has helped you when you felt like you were not good enough in the relationship?

In what ways has she let you know she does not feel good enough for you?

If you had to guess, where do you think she feels like she is not good enough or disappointing?

What did you know about body image and self-confidence and how it affects sexual desire?

How do you think societal messages have affected your relationship?

How can you help rebuild her confidence in knowing she can have wants and needs about sex?

In what ways do you think you have contributed to her feelings of not being good enough about her body or sex?

How do you think you can help adjust the message so that she knows she is good enough?

Shame About Sex

She can also struggle with shame that can come from wanting too much sex or not enough sex, and this can be learned from childhood and cultural messages.[111] Sometimes this feeling of shame can be hard to overcome, even if she does not feel she should hold it. Shame can lead to self-objectification about her body, which results in lower self-esteem and lower overall satisfaction with life.[112] Shame can be hard to overcome and is something that is easier to work on with a partner so they can be a support when that feeling arises. Shame is often internalized due to all those mixed messages that she was given as she was growing up, so it doesn't feel good no matter which decision she makes about sex. As we talked about earlier, she is made to feel bad about wanting sex or not wanting sex, so she feels that she just can't win. Let's talk more about this challenge that she faces.

Women can feel shame for either declining or wanting to have sex. When she has a desire for sex, it can be seen as wrong and impure. The message is that only men want sex, not women—at least not women who have good morals, who are good girls, and who are not whores or rebels. So, starting in adolescence, women are implicitly and explicitly taught by parents and society to suppress that desire, and then they are shamed for not having enough desire when they get married and do not want to have sex all the time.[113] So women are taught that it is both wrong to want sex and to not want sex. Huh?

---

111 Fahs et al., 2020.
112 Mercurio & Landry, 2008; Sævik & Konijnenberg, 2023.
113 Fahs et al., 2020.

Sexual shame is messaged to women through society, culture, and gendered expectations that are internalized and result in maladaptive thoughts, beliefs, and behaviors about being a sexual being and having sexual needs or desires.[114] As sexual urges first begin to appear in adolescence, women are taught that these urges are wrong, and if they are not careful, they will make men do bad things to them, so they should hold back their sexual desires, thus developing a sense of shame around anything to do with sexual urges.[115] What a confusing message to receive. First it is not okay to want sex, and you shouldn't ever have that desire. Then, when you are married, you should set aside all those things that have been pounded into your brain, and suddenly sex is expected as long as it is satisfying your husband's needs. They are not taught that it is natural and it is okay to explore their bodies and find out what it is that they like so when they are eventually with a partner, they can have a fun sexual relationship. Actually, they can be in trouble for talking about sex, being caught masturbating, and reading books that have sexual themes. They are made to feel like they are doing something wrong, or in some cases that they are going to hell for their desires. The only thing that is socially acceptable for women is romance, not sex.

She may struggle with accepting that it is okay to have desires and that wanting sex is perfectly natural for her. Instead, you'll find that she puts herself down, body shames, or is even hostile to herself for wanting sex, and on the flip side she feels shame for not wanting sex, because she should

---

114 Sævik & Konijnenberg, 2023.
115 Dinse et al., 2023.

be pleasing her partner, feeling ashamed about how her body looks, and feeling inferior. She might even feel she is defective because she cannot make her partner happy.[116] Society tells adolescent girls that sex is shameful and bad, and then people wonder why women struggle with letting go and enjoying their sexual desires. Women do not typically know how to follow their pleasure and just be in the moment to enjoy sex, as their head is filled with conflicting messages that are hard to untangle. It is difficult to figure out which messages they want to keep and which they can discard. Instead, she is usually trying to make two contradictory messages be true, which isn't possible and can result in negative sexual outcomes for the relationship.

---

116 Sævik & Konijnenberg, 2023.

REFLECTION 7.3: Shame About Sex

When you think back on messages you received about sex growing up, what were they?

_____

_____

_____

_____

_____

Do your messages and women's messages about sex seem to differ? How?

_____

_____

_____

_____

If you had these two conflicting messages about sex, how might it affect you?

_____

_____

_____

_____

What have you learned about the shame women feel about sex?

_____

_____

_____

_____

What impact does knowing about the conflicting messages around sex have on you?

What changes can you make to help her untangle the messages and shame?

Chapter 8

How Do Swirling Thoughts Affect Her?

Hard to Stay Present

Hopefully, in the process of reading the chapters of this book so far, you've come to see that there is a lot going on in her head before it even becomes a physical action. Perhaps there is greater understanding being gained of how these thoughts affect mental load at almost all times of the day. Unfortunately, this mental work can't be switched off and ignored whenever she wants, as it is within her and feels urgent.

Women have to alter how they think about their lives once they become mothers. It is no longer only about what they want in life, but about what is best for the life of the child in their care. Women still have high caregiver ideology, while men still have breadwinner ideology, even if both are working full-time.[117] Even if both of you are working full-time, she typically tends to be the one who still figures out the schedule for kids, determines how to get them places, leaves work early if they need to be sent home, and overall holds the ownership of all things involving caretaking with children. Even schools will usually call the mother's phone number first for issues with children and call the father's number only after being unable to reach the mother.

Research has shown that parenting stress and unequal division of household and mental labor are associated with lower sexual desire and dissatisfaction with emotional connection in the relationship.[118] It is hard to desire sex when her ideology is all about ensuring someone else's survival and well-being first. If it feels as though she is the only one in the relationship who will think about all the things that need to be considered, then she will do it, but it will come with a cost to the relationship, and that usually is a sexual cost and sometimes an emotional connection cost, both of which affect the relationship negatively.

The stress and mental load that come with taking care of children can be high, and it is all on her. Without feeling there is enough support, there will be a lower desire for sex. It becomes lower on the priority list as her mental and emotional capacity is drained, and there is not a feeling of being valued for this unpaid labor.[119] Certain duties and needs must be prioritized, and it would appear for the majority of women that, once children are in the picture,

---

117 Bataille & Hyland, 2023.
118 Harris et al., 2022.
119 Harris et al., 2022.

sexual desire often goes to the bottom of the list until there is more room for it. Sex doesn't have the same urgency as keeping a child alive, supported, and emotionally safe, so sex doesn't reach as high on the priority list.

As children get older, there is an expectation that they will help with the daily chores, but in most homes this is not what happens, and it feels unfair to the woman.[120] She may struggle with feeling used when there are people in the home who are capable of helping out with all the things that seem to fall on her plate, yet no one has the initiative to do anything. Then she starts to feel like a nag when she has to constantly ask for help that seems so obvious. Remember the poem from chapter one? This is where she can see all the things that need to be done, and it is hurtful that it is all left to her to do when others in the family see the need but choose to do nothing because they know she will take care of it. All the mess isn't hers, but no one else feels the need to pick up after themselves without being asked. She doesn't want to be a nag yet also doesn't want to be the only one taking care of the obvious.

As discussed in depth, the executive functioning system plays an important role in affecting how much room is in her head, how fatigued she is with making decisions, and how emotionally drained she is, leading to whether her mind has capacity and space for desire for sex. Compounding that huge daily mental drain is whether she is feeling emotionally connected and safe with her partner, and whether it feels like he is on her side. If she is alone, this will also

---

120 Sarmiento et al., 2024.

affect the priority for sex at the end of the day. When she feels like she is in a partnership instead of having another person she has to manage, this affects whether she thinks she is desirous and sexy or just a mom and caretaker. The constant thoughts, fears, worries, agendas, and decisions rolling around in her head make it a challenge for sex to be at the forefront of the mind without his help.

Sometimes she wants to have sex, but it is hard to stay present in the moment. Thoughts will invade her mind with checklists and things that must get done, and suddenly she is on a thought train that she didn't want to be on. It is hard to enjoy a sexual activity when your mind is taking you away from the present moment into that never-ending obligations space. It is like the mental load has a constant tug for her attention and doesn't care if she wants to focus on something else instead. This can happen to her even during the day with things that are not sex. It can be quite frustrating. Maybe she is trying to get particular tasks completed, but every time she moves, she sees another thing that can be done, so she does that "quickly," which distracts from what she was working on, and suddenly she has spent a whole day doing a lot of things, but nothing is completed, so it looks like she didn't do anything.

This constant thought train with mental load tugging for attention and seeming more urgent than what she is currently doing is why many women struggle to relax at home. There is always something that requires her attention instead of the relaxing activity that she wants to do. Due to the guilt or shame that comes from feeling obligated to take care of everyone, she can feel like she is wasting her time relaxing or that she doesn't deserve it yet. Even though, as we've talked about earlier, many of the things she is responsible for are Groundhog Day things, so there is no true completion of them. This can make it hard to relax, because there is always something that could be accomplished instead of her self-care, which internally doesn't feel as high a priority as everything else.

There are so many layers to why thoughts can be swirling in her head, and the mental load was just one of them. "Societal pressure" thoughts can also affect her thought processes. She could be struggling with thinking about how she looks while having sex. This self-criticism can make it hard for some women to want to have sex with the lights on or with being able to see themselves or even thinking that their partner can see them while engaging in sexual activities, because she worries about how she looks and doesn't feel sexy or think that she is attractive enough for you. Societal pressure also gives her worry or stress about whether she is having sex too often or not enough to be considered a good wife and not be thought of as a slut or whore. There is a lot of shame around being either too interested in sex or not interested enough. While at the same time she is concerned about whether it is sex because she is a sex doll—and that is what he thinks she is good for—or because he actually loves her and enjoys being with her intimately, whether sex is involved or not, and this can make her want sex more often, because then she feels it is about her and not her vagina. See how the thoughts swirl and become so tangled that it can be confusing and hard to focus? It can be difficult to stay present and enjoy the moment when she isn't even sure whether she should be ashamed or feel guilty at that moment, let alone having fun.

Add another layer of knowing whether she actually wants to have sex or if she is agreeing to it because she feels like she has to, because otherwise she might lose your emotional connection. Sometimes she can become so detached from feeling her body that she isn't even sure what she truly wants and what she is just going along with, which can then become a source of frustration because she isn't sure if she is wholly consenting to sex or just doing it to be a good spouse. This layer can be truly confusing when she isn't connected enough to herself to even know what she really wants at the moment.

Then there can be a fear that a child might walk in, wake up, or hear the sexual activity, and this has its own layer of anxieties. She wants to be available for the child if they need her and is worried about being "caught" in a sexual activity and not knowing how she would explain it to the child, or she is afraid that she will make the child uncomfortable if they hear the sounds from sexual activities. Some of these worries can stem from societal messages and also can come from her experiences in childhood or stories she hears from other people.

Any one or more of these layers could be affecting her ability to stay present in the moment during a sexual encounter. It is not to say that every single one of these things discussed will be running through her mind every single time she is attempting to engage in a sexual activity with you, but it is any one or combination of these things that could pop into her mind, and she loses focus as the thought train whisks her away. Many times it is the mental load that has the greatest impact, as it is such a near-constant part of her thoughts. She wants to be with you and enjoy being with you and—*POP!*—in comes a thought about signing a paper, completing a project, remembering to take something out of the freezer for the next day, making a doctor appointment, or texting someone back about a playdate, and immediately her mind is out of the present moment and on the mental load instead.

REFLECTION 8.1: Swirling Thoughts

Have you ever experienced swirling thoughts while trying to do something else? Explain.

How does it affect you to learn how pervasive these thoughts can be to her?

What did you know about her taking on responsibilities with children even if both adults are working?What do you think now about responsibilities with children even if both parents are working?

What swirling thoughts had you not considered would be happening for her?

What swirling thoughts do you think your partner deals with the most?

In what ways do you think these thoughts affect her ability to stay in the present with you?

How do you think societal messages get in the way of sexual experiences?

Part 3:

What Can You Do?

Chapter 9

How to Become More Egalitarian

Egalitarian What?

What does an egalitarian relationship even mean? An egalitarian relationship is when partners are sharing the responsibilities for the family in a more equal way based on mutual respect for each other and what the strengths are for each person, regardless of gender. Included in this equality is unpaid labor like household chores and taking care of children, as well as the paid labor of financial responsibilities and how they are shared in a way that feels fair to both people and does not have to be based on traditional gender roles.

This means that in an egalitarian relationship, the woman could be the breadwinner and the man could be the primary caretaker for children and unpaid labor at home if that is what works best for this couple. It also means that both people can be doing paid work and also splitting the unpaid work at home in a manner that doesn't feel unequal. In essence, both people get to clock out of unpaid labor each day, and it doesn't all fall to one person to be on 24/7, whether they are contributing with paid labor or not. These couples are sharing the mental load, and when both take on parts of this invisible load, it is spread between two people instead of one person bearing it all. There is not a one-size-fits-all for an egalitarian relationship; rather, it is about having conversations and finding ways that both people can feel they are doing a fair share of the unpaid labor in the family, and that could look different for different relationships. These types of relationships are built on equal power, respect for one another, and friendship with each other, allowing for connection both physically and emotionally so both benefit from the partnership.

To work toward an egalitarian relationship, both people will have to do some work initially. She will have to learn to give up some control and trust that you will do the things you say you will be responsible for in the way that works best for you, which may not look exactly like how she would do it. You will have to learn how to take on the mental load and what it truly means to own a task fully, as you haven't had this practice at home, maybe ever, and it is a skill that must be practiced. The couple will have to have conversations and be open and honest with each other so that they can work toward an equal partnership that feels beneficial and fair to both people.

Wow, that is a lot to take in. You can sit on that for a minute if you need to so you can process what changes may need to be made in your relationship—and by you specifically—to work toward this type of relationship. The thing I want you to hear is that this will be work that both of you need to do together. It isn't about you making all the changes to please her, but how you two can work together and partner to make the relationship work feel more equal for both of you.

Egalitarian relationships are higher-quality relationships because partners are communicating more together and developing real cooperation with each other, which allows for a healthy sexual and marital relationship.[121] With what you've learned in all the previous chapters in this book, you will be coming to this conversation with much more knowledge than you had before. Now you can use that knowledge to have a more understanding conversation that will hopefully encourage growth and closer connection for both of you. Next, we are going to go over what adds and takes away from the mental load so that your work of taking more of it on will be beneficial and so that you don't accidentally think you are doing it, only to find out later that you aren't actually providing the relief you think you are. This is the progression from being a helper to being an equal partner.

---

121 Carlson et al., 2018.

REFLECTION 9.1: Egalitarian What?

What do you think about working toward an egalitarian relationship now that you know what it means?

What feels different about this type of relationship that you hadn't considered before?

What would be the hardest part for you about growing into this type of relationship?

Where would you want to grow and change to go toward equality and fairness?

What fears do you have about this change with your partner?

How does this type of open and honest conversation sit with you? Any fears?

How can you bring this conversation up with your partner so that it is a meaningful one and doesn't feel like an attack for either of you?

What Adds to the Mental Load?

It would probably be helpful to learn about what adds to the mental load that she is dealing with constantly—and for which she needs you to bear the burden more equally. You know what it is now, and all the things she might have running through her head. You also know that men have been in a transition time where they *want* to help with it but don't know how to take it on without being told *where* to help. Maybe you have offered to help your partner and said something to indicate that you are available to help and just need to be told what to do, and she may have responded with something that lets you go and not help instead of telling you what to do, or she may say something about not wanting to have to tell you what to do. Why might this happen when you want to help and just need to know what needs to be done?

Having to tell someone else how to help or write out a list of things to do actually adds to her mental load. It becomes another thing she has to think about in an already overwhelmed executive functioning system, and she may not have the energy to give you that information even though she desperately wants your help. Many times women get upset at this point because they think about how no one tells them what needs to be done or how to help, but they look around, see the need, and jump in to take care of it.

Men usually did not grow up learning these skills and were always told what to do to help, and then they would do it, even if it was grudgingly, because it was interrupting the thing they wanted to be doing instead. They were not taught to take care of things by looking around and just doing it.

Many times, they also do not care as much about the same things women do, so it doesn't feel as urgent to take care of something. So, while she may be upset that she has to give you a list or guidance, you probably need to practice the skill of how to manage things on your own without input from her first. This takes a lot of practice, but it will become a more natural feeling after a while if you stick with it. The following table can give you some guidance that doesn't add to her mental load.

QUESTION YOU WANT TO ASK ABOUT	ADDS TO THE MENTAL LOAD—ALL ON HER	DOESN'T ADD TO THE MENTAL LOAD—COLLABORATIVE
Going to the grocery store	I am happy to go to the grocery store for you today. Can you write me a list of what you want me to pick up?	I noticed we need some things from the grocery store, so I will stop by there today. Here is the list I have made of the things I know we need, and please let me know if there is anything specific you want me to pick up.
Dropping off / picking up kids for extracurricular activities	I can drop off / pick up the kid from their activity. What time do I need to get them? Where is it? Do I need to bring anything? What do I need to do?	I can drop off / pick up the kid from their activity at ___ p.m. I looked up the location, so I know where to go, and I saw that it is their week to bring a snack to share, so I will stop at the store and pick up ___ snack for them all. Is there anything else I need to know that I haven't checked on already?

Helping around the house	I am happy to help around the house. Just tell me what to do and I will do it.	I noticed a basket of laundry that needed to be folded and put away, so I went ahead and did that task. I saw that the dishwasher needed to be unloaded, so I took care of that and put everything away where it goes. I also noticed the kitchen and dining room floors needed cleaning, so I swept them and will be able to mop tonight. I want to communicate with you that these tasks were taken care of. If they were on your mind to do, you can check them off now.

Table 9.1: Examples of Ways to Help That
Add or Don't Add to the Mental Load

Adding to the mental load gives her more work around thinking, processing, and either speaking or writing out what she wants you to do. It makes sense that you think that you are helping when you ask her to let you help her, because you want to support her and not leave everything to her. It also makes sense that she gets frustrated, because she needs you to be able to act without direction so there is equal brain energy being spent on the tasks. This is where working on communal strength can come in, as both of you are able to meet in the middle, with you doing what you think should be done and finding answers on your own, and then checking in to provide a space for her to collaborate with you if there is more to it.

In the table above, you can see that just asking her to write a list, gather all the information for you, or tell you what household tasks need to be accomplished will all add to her mental load. Now she has to stop what she may have been working on to think about and process what groceries need to be picked up or look up and find information to relay to you. Sure, she may know where or how to get the requested information for you, but when she does that, she has to stop in the tab she is looking at in her mind to go find the tab in her head with that information. Thinking about where to find that information can distract her from the task she was occupied with, and it can be hard to get back to the tab she was working in. This extra energy required from her is why sometimes she will seem like she doesn't want your help, as it is adding to her mental load, when in actuality she does want your help, but she wants it in a way that detracts from her mental load instead of adding to it.

REFLECTION 9.2: Adds to the Mental Load

How do you see questions asking your partner how you can help as adding to her mental load now?

From table 9.1, what do you notice is the biggest difference in helping her?

In what ways do you now notice you add to her mental load when you are wanting to help?

What makes sense now about her frustration when you really want to help her out?

What kind of practice do you think you need to be able to take on more of the mental load?

What Detracts from the Mental Load?

To have a more egalitarian relationship, you will begin to partner more equitably with her so that you are an equal instead of a step below her, waiting to be told what to do around the home or with the children. You can look around and notice tasks that need to be done and do them without being told. Essentially, you get rid of the honey-do list of old times and equally figure out what needs to be done so the burden of remembering everything no longer falls solely on her.[122]

What detracts from the mental load is not giving her more decisions to make, asking for her knowledge when you could find out for yourself, or wanting her to tell you what to do. It is easy to go to her because it seems like she has all the answers and knows all that needs to be done, so why do it for yourself? However, it creates more decision, mental, and emotional fatigue for her as she becomes overwhelmed. Being able to work together, collaboratively, on unpaid labor increases the feeling of teamwork the couple has with each other.[123] When you start figuring things out without the lists or using her as your search engine for information, then her various fatigues can be lowered, and she won't feel so overwhelmed by everything. Instead of allowing her to feel responsible for all the unpaid labor, you pick up and carry that responsibility with her so there is a more equal distribution.[124]

Conversations are important because equity doesn't

---

122 Ahn et al., 2017.
123 Carlson et al., 2018.
124 Ahn et al., 2017.

necessarily mean equal division of the labor. Sharing unpaid labor can affect the relationship positively in that the perception of fairness and satisfaction between the couple is met.[125] So talking with each other honestly and openly about working together to take responsibility for the mental load and other unpaid responsibilities in the family will be beneficial to your overall relationship satisfaction. Next we are going to talk about what it looks like to take ownership of responsibilities in a way that spreads the mental load more equitably.

---

125 Ohlsson-Wijk et al., 2022.

REFLECTION 9.3: Detracts from the Mental Load

How often do you look around and notice what needs to be done now?

What kind of change would that be for you to start noticing and acting without a list?

How could you team up with her on unpaid labor responsibilities more?

How would you approach having an open conversation with her to collaborate on equity?

Chapter 10

How to Take Ownership and Responsibility of Tasks

Taking full ownership and responsibility of tasks may be a newer idea for you. You may be used to doing the work that is asked of you, so you are a good helper, but maybe you don't know what it would look like to take *full* ownership of tasks from beginning to end. It would encompass the mental load and the physical labor of the task, which might feel weird at first. You would do the planning, thinking, and writing, and then the doing for the task—whatever that might be without your partner initiating your action in the task. You might even feel a little bit of defensiveness here, because you feel like you do a lot, and somehow this section is saying that you do not do as much as you feel you do.

Let's slow down for a minute and take a deep breath. This section is not to negate all that you do already. It is to help you become more of an equal and secure partner with this

24/7 mental load that never rests, so that it is no longer all on one person in the relationship but is being balanced by both of you. You are going to level up from a helper to an initiator, creating a second partner who is at the same level, affecting your relationship dynamic in a positive way. So breathe. This is a good thing, and the defensive part of you that wants to protect you and say that you do good things isn't needed, because we know you do good things. We are going to help you get to the next level so you can do even better.

Weaponized Incompetence

First, let's talk about something we want to make sure you are not doing. Weaponized incompetence is detrimental to a relationship. It sometimes is referred to as strategic incompetence, but it means the same thing.[126] This may or may not be a phrase you have heard before. What does weaponized incompetence mean? It is a strategy a person uses to avoid responsibility by passive-aggressively doing a task badly and then claiming that their partner is better at it, or they don't understand how to do it well, even if they have been shown how to do it multiple times.[127] It causes harm to the relationship because it creates an imbalance with the mental and emotional labors between the partners, as one person feels responsible for managing all parts of the family's life, including and mostly for childcare and housework, and the other person is able to do what they want without care.

---

126 Wong, 2022.
127 Wong, 2022.

These are not stupid people, but they would rather pretend to be stupid, or incompetent, about something because they have no interest in doing the task.[128] The point is that if they do the task poorly enough or create enough frustration for their partner in having to explain the steps for the task every single time, and then they still mess it up because "they just can't figure it out," then the partner will give up and do it themselves. This is ultimately the end goal for weaponized incompetence: to get out of doing tasks that the person doesn't want to do and not be bothered with being asked to do them again in the future so that they do not have to feel an emotion about not doing it. They are justifying that they do not do that task so they do not feel an emotion like guilt, shame, or embarrassment over the fact that they are pretending to themselves and to their partner that they are unable to figure out how to complete a task. They will use phrases like the following:

- You are just so much better at this than me.
- You already have all the information in your head, so why don't you just do it, because it'll be faster?
- This feels more like your thing, because you're better at the details.
- I won't do it to your standards, so why don't you just do it?
- I did it badly last time, so you should just do it this time.
- I can do it, but I am so slow that it will take me three times as long as it would take you to do it, but I'll do it.

---

128 Hax, 2024.

- This is your area of expertise; you are just so good at it.
- If I do it, I will mess it up and do it wrong.

This is not an exhaustive list, but I wanted you to get an idea of what it sounds like. The main ideas here are either trying to make the other person feel like they are so good and the only one that is competent in doing it, or that they are going to do it, but it is not going to end well. There are always going to be those tasks that you don't want to do, but is it fair to leave everything to her to do simply because you don't want to do it? Is that partnership or more like a parent–child relationship? In the book *Fair Play* by Eve Rodsky, she goes over all the tasks that have to be done and talks about them as cards. She even has task cards that couples can buy to fairly distribute between each other to visualize the tasks and to see, out of one hundred tasks that need to be completed, how many cards are you holding—five, ten, twelve? That means that those other tasks still have to be done, and if you won't do them, then she *has* to even if she hates those tasks as much as you do. In that same book, it is discussed how parenting your husband is not sexy, nor is the need to constantly praise him for doing the bare minimum.

This happens a lot with men who are using weaponized incompetence in a relationship. Sandy asks Mark to clean the kitchen so that she can take care of other tasks that day. He only loads the dishwasher and he does it poorly. He stacks things on top of each other and doesn't put the silverware in the holder correctly so that nothing will actually get clean in this load of dishes. Then he fills the pot with water and leaves it in the sink and does not wipe down any of the counters or sweep the floors. While it usually takes Sandy two hours to clean the kitchen, Mark is feeling done after only fifteen minutes. He sits on the couch and starts scrolling through his phone and watching TV. Sandy walks by as she is rushing around trying to take care of five other tasks at the same time. She sees him sitting on the couch and comes to a halt. She looks into the kitchen and sees that some work has been done, but it is by no means clean yet.

SANDY: What are you doing? Please, will you finish cleaning the kitchen?!

MARK: (Looks up from his phone.) I already finished cleaning the kitchen.

SANDY: That is not a clean kitchen, Mark. All you did was get some stuff out of the sink. She walks over to the dishwasher and opens it up to look inside. She sees how haphazardly he has loaded it and sighs away her frustration. She thinks: *Why do I even ask him to help me around the house? He never does it well and always does it at 50 percent so that there is still more work for me to do. It's like he doesn't even care that he is leaving me to feel alone in the work and that I can't trust him to be there for me. I have told him many times how to load the dishwasher correctly so that it actually cleans the dishes! Ugh!* Mark, please come here.

MARK: *Okay, she saw that the dishwasher wasn't loaded correctly again. I'll have to ask her to show me how to load it correctly again, 'cause, damn, I just can't seem to figure this one out. Hopefully, this time she will learn to just stop asking me to help clean the kitchen. Aside from taking out the garbage, I shouldn't be cleaning the kitchen. It shouldn't be a job I have to help with. I hate that chore. Actually, I hate all chores. Why do I have to help with anything around the house? Why can't she just take care of me like she does the house and kids too?* I am coming, just a sec.

SANDY: Mark, this isn't how you load a dishwasher. How many times have I shown you how to do it?

MARK: Yeah, I know, I am just not as good at it as you. You are so much better than me. Whenever I try, I just don't do as good a job as you do.

SANDY: I really need your help here. I can't do everything. *I don't understand. He is so good at so many other things and can figure out such complex tech, but loading the dishwasher is too complicated for him?* I am just one person in a house with four people. I am running myself ragged and would love to have some time to just sit around and do nothing, but I can't because if I don't do all the tasks, then we wouldn't have clothes to wear, food to eat, and there would be filth everywhere. Where is your initiative? Why can't you figure out how to do something as simple as load a dishwasher properly or clean a kitchen well? It involves wiping down counters, sweeping floors, and scrubbing pots, which you did none of today. Please, can you show up for me?

MARK: Okay, I'm sorry. *Damn, she seems really upset. I think I need to actually help her out. She looks like she is getting worn down.*

People who use weaponized incompetence in relationships think they are winning, but really they are losing. Their partner is slowly giving up on them, and then they give up on their relationship. They are being negatively affected every day as they are overwhelmed by constant tasks, knowing they are the only one who will do most of them, so they feel isolated and are developing a lack of trust in their supposed life partner. There is a distinct imbalance in the relationship, as one person is overfunctioning because the other person is underfunctioning.[129] As one person does less, the other has to pick up the slack and do more, so eventually one person only does tasks they want to do, and the other does everything else whether they enjoy the task or hate it. They are being taught how to be alone and do everything on their own, and then their partner always feels blindsided when they decide they want a divorce because it would be easier to live on their own. Weaponized incompetence is creating conflict, mistrust, and relationship dissatisfaction where there doesn't need to be any. This is such an easy thing to fix, because it is simply this person deciding to show up for the other person.

Weaponized incompetence is a persistent inability to learn despite ample opportunities of being taught and shown how to do a task. This person is stuck in a loop of failure that

---

129 Wong, 2022.

they don't seem interested in breaking out of. They have competence in many other areas that they are *interested* in and are able to grow in those areas, while they are unable to gain competence in other areas that they have *no interest* in, so there is a refusal to learn or grow, and the incompetence (a.k.a. stupidity) only appears in tasks they want to avoid. The tasks they are avoiding are usually menial and not hard to learn, so the fact that they are incompetent in these tasks, like how to load a dishwasher or how to start a load of laundry, shows an unwillingness to be an equal partner in the relationship, which is why it hurts it so much and can eventually lead to divorce.

What do you do if you think you might be unconsciously using weaponized incompetence? As I said earlier, it is an easy thing to fix. You make the decision that you are not going to be lazy about learning how to do something anymore. You decide that your partner means more to you than the fact that you hate doing some chore. Just like when you want to learn how to do anything else in life, you go online to Google or YouTube and watch videos or read articles and learn how to do things properly, and then you practice and do it until you gain the skill in it.[130] You refuse to say things like "You are just better at it than me . . . why don't you do it?" and instead you say that you are going to do it over again so that you can learn from your mistakes and do it better next time.

If you are using weaponized incompetence consciously, then you need to ask yourself if you enjoy being married.

---

130 Rathner, 2024.

One day she will decide enough is enough and leave. If you like having sex, then this isn't a good tactic either. There is absolutely nothing sexy about a man pretending to be incompetent at something menial like housework or important like taking care of children. Overall this is a losing life strategy, and you will end up alone, so do not try this, and if you are doing it, give it up.

The funny thing is, she is telling you exactly what she is looking for, and if you listen, then you don't have to guess about what it takes to do the job well. You wouldn't even have to pull up videos to learn how to do it right, because she has probably given you that information many times over, and all you have to do is listen. Sure, you may hate the task at hand, but do you really think she loves it, or does she hate it just as much? Isn't sometimes being a grown-up figuring out how to work together to get a job done even when neither of you want to do it? The interesting part is that when you do a job really well, without having to be reminded or nagged, it is so relieving and feels so good to her that you look good in her eyes. The more effort you put in, the better you look, and the better you look, the more adult you look and the sexier you look. The opposite is true with weaponized incompetence—you just look infantile, which is not sexy.

REFLECTION 10.1: Weaponized Incompetence

In what areas do you think you may have unconsciously (or consciously) used weaponized incompetence with housework or childcare?

Have there been times you have asked your partner to show you multiple times how to do something and still done it poorly? Explain.

What makes it challenging to share with your partner what tasks you would like to do and which ones you do not want to do so that you can both find a balance in tasks?

Have you ever used the weaponized incompetence phrases to get out of doing a task? Explain.

Starting today, what are you going to do now to ensure you become competent in areas you have been incompetent in?

Equality in Responsibilities for Unpaid Labor

For a long time in our society, men went to work and women stayed home. Men did manual labor or worked in offices, and women raised children and cleaned the house. Men punched in and out of a clock, and women worked 24/7, and that was just accepted by all as how life goes. Times slowly began to change, and women started entering the workforce, going to college, and sharing the same world as men, yet they were still expected to stay fully in their world as well. Women learned that their world was a lot more than men's and had much higher expectations, and they started wanting men to meet them in their world a little more too. They wanted help with housework and childcare. They wanted more equality with what had to happen in daily life so it felt more fair between the two grown adults who were supposed to be partners.

At this era in our society, it has been found that there are three types of ideologies men can have about their role in the family. There is the traditional role of the breadwinner, the transitional role of still mostly focusing on being the breadwinner but also attempting to be a nurturing parent, and the egalitarian role that is present for paid and unpaid labors but prioritizes caregiving.[131] Traditionals do not see themselves as needing to be involved with caregiving and leave that to women, because they are better at it, so they can focus on providing financially for the family. Transitionals are the in-between males who still primarily focus on providing financially for the family but also allow some

---

131 Bataille & Hyland, 2023.

space to show up for their children in a nurturing way. Egalitarians have figured out how to provide financial support for their family but do not allow it to be their primary focus and instead encompass active caregiving to their children and spouse as their priority.[132]

You will see the traditionals as the guys who use weaponized incompetence because they refuse to learn how to wash a dish, load a washing machine, or change a diaper so their spouse will stop asking them to do it. These guys believe that their only job is to go to work and make money, and her job is everything else. The problem is that he would be going to work whether he was in a relationship or not, so it really is the bare minimum that he can be doing, and that just isn't enough anymore. There is too much to do and to think about for one person, and she needs help. So the bare minimum doesn't cut it when she can have a job to make money and do all the things herself, too, and just not have him in the picture, which ultimately ends up being easier if he isn't helping, because then she doesn't have to clean up after him too. Then he doesn't get why she leaves him and doesn't want to be with him when he was such a big help by bringing home the bacon.

The problem is that he doesn't see how that isn't as much help as he thinks it is. The mental and unpaid labors are so much higher and taxing than his clock-in-and-out-of job, and hopefully, at this point, you understand more about this and have more empathy. You get that being a traditional guy and doing the bare minimum of going to work and bringing

---

132 Bataille & Hyland, 2023.

home a paycheck isn't enough to help with the mental load and equally distribute that and the unpaid labors around the house.

The transitionals are where many guys are now in our society. They get that they can't just bring home a paycheck and expect her to bring him a drink while he sits on the couch. Life isn't slow enough for that anymore; there is way too much going on now. They understand that they need to be involved in parenting and help out around the house more. The problem is that they don't yet have the initiative to do it the way she does it. They don't know how to look around and see what needs to be done and just start doing things, or to collaborate with her by starting a conversation about what needs to be done.

Instead, they are the guys who wait for the honey-do list or ask how they can help. They want to show up for her; they just need to be told what to do. Unfortunately, these guys don't realize that this just adds to her mental load. Now she has to think about what she wants done, what he might be willing to do, and what will get the least resistance from him, then write it out for him. It is a lot of decision-making on someone who could already be facing decision fatigue. Sometimes she doesn't have the mental energy to give him that list or ask for that help, so he thinks that she doesn't need anything from him, when in actuality she is desperate for his help but needs him to take initiative and collaborate with her, not wait for her to hand him a list.

This is where the egalitarians come in and have leveled up in the relationship. These are the guys other spouses meet and then jokingly ask if they teach classes or if they have any brothers. They know how to help their partner without being asked, they have initiative, and they respond to children's cries or messes they see. These guys take on a share of the mental load so that it isn't all on her, and they own the part they take on. These are the men who believe that no one should be working 24/7, and they want to equally share the unpaid labor with their partner so both of them can rest. For example, if his wife was up most of the night with the baby because he/she couldn't sleep, then he gets up with the baby in the morning and lets her sleep for as long as she can, and he takes care of everything for the baby, without bothering her, that she would normally do—feeding, washing, dressing (in clothes that fit and match, no incompetence here), playing, talking, and arranging for a sitter—until she is ready to tag in. He doesn't expect a reward for it or make a big deal out of it. He does it because it is how he shows her that they are on the same team, and since she handled so much labor throughout the night, he can handle the morning so she can sleep in, and this is just fair in his mind.

In this egalitarian relationship, both of them would thank each other for things like taking care of housework and childcare and how appreciative they are that they help each other with these things, but the key is that it is *both* of them. In the other two types, the guy rarely if ever acknowledges all that she does, but he always expects recognition anytime he does anything, which is extremely unbalanced. In egalitarian relationships, the respect and recognition for unpaid labor goes both ways. This is because he is cognizant of all that is required to make the visible things happen and understands there is so much more that is happening that is mostly invisible. Check out the table below on what he knows is associated with picking up a child from soccer practice.

FINDING A SPORT	REGISTERING	PREPPING	CALENDAR
• Research leagues in the area • Research what kind of league would be best for your kid • Look into how to enroll (might include emails, website searches, phone calls) • Set reminder on phone or calendar to register on specified day	• Take them to doctor's office for sports vaccines or physicals to be allowed to register • Remember to register them on the day • Fill out all the paperwork to register them • Find where practices and games will be held	• Find out what uniform is needed for the child to wear during practice and during games • Take the child to try on a uniform and shoes, then buy the uniform before first practice (If ordering online, order with enough time that it gets to them to try on to find out if it fits) • Wash the uniform and have it ready to go for the first practice and every practice/game thereafter	• Add location and time for every practice and game to the calendar • Plan meals around practices/ games so they can be there • Plan vacations around the sport's schedule • Prepare everything needed to get to practice/ game on time (snack/drink/ uniforms/ activities for other kids)

Table 10.1: Mental Load for Child in a Sport

So when she asks him to pick up their child from soccer practice, he has done his job of making sure he also knows where and when the practices/games will be held so that he can participate. He will not have to stop the flow and ask her what time or where or what the child needs. He will know where they keep the athletic bag and how to access the family calendar, which holds vital information like times and locations. She feels like she has an actual life partner who is equal to her and can be trusted and relied on with everyday things.

How do you become egalitarian? It is about sharing the mental load and owning parts of it in a way that she can fully trust that you will take care of things so that she no longer has to think about them anymore, thereby allowing these things to no longer be a part of her mental load. In this way the burden becomes shared instead of all on one person, which frees up room in her head to think about other things in life, like what she might want. She can also see you as an adult and not another person in her life she has to take care of each day, which is sexy instead of desexualizing. One of the things to begin to do is make sure that you are sharing information so that you do not have to go to her to ask about things. For places that will email only one of you, have a shared email address so you both can easily access the information. Places that might do this would be the child's school or doctor's office. Table 10.2 provides ideas for information sharing so this information can be accessible by both of you.

Ways to Share So Information Is Easily Accessible to Both

A shared family email address for all things that have to do with the kids' school, extracurricular activities, doctor appointments/ information, or shared appointments between the both of you.

Grocery list in kitchen that both can add to as they see something that needs to be picked up (or for the one who is not owning that responsibility to write what they need).

Shared calendar—electronic or paper—that holds information about who has what going on each day so no single person is responsible for being the information keeper.

A book with websites and passwords that either can access as needed so it isn't on one person to remember all the passwords.

Finance apps to make the budget visible to both people, even if one is responsible for it (Monarch is a great app for this).

Table 10.2: Information Sharing Ideas

After you have created systems for making information accessible to both of you, make sure that you are actually accessing them. Yes, she probably knows a lot of the answers you have, but it matters so much that you find the answers for yourself instead of having her stop and find them for you. If you can't remember what time something is happening, pull up the calendar first and look there; then, if you can't find the information, you can say that you checked the shared calendar and don't see the information you are looking for, and does she know where you should look to find the answer? This shows that you are putting in effort before going to her, and that matters. It can sometimes take a little bit to work the bugs out of a system, but if you both stick with it and communicate about what is working and what is not, then those bugs will get worked through and the systems will function properly. Both of you will know how to access information, and she will not be your home Google anymore, alleviating a lot of stress and mental fatigue on her and helping you to feel confident and competent in what is happening at home.

The next part is owning responsibilities fully. This means taking accountability for all the mental load and actionable parts of tasks. If you need more help with this, Eve Rodsky does an amazing job explaining how to do this in her book *Fair Play*, and I highly recommend both of you reading it and then using her cards to help divide up responsibilities in the home in what feels fair to your relationship. This means you don't just help your partner out by taking the kiddo to a playdate but actually take ownership of playdates sometimes. Do you know what goes into setting up a playdate for a child? Let's look at the next chart and see what is involved with setting up a playdate, then think about how many steps you have been involved with in the past.

- Contacting the parent of the child you want to set up a play-date with.
- Finding dates and times that work with both schedules.
- Finding a location that will work for children and adults.
- Multiplying this step exponentially with each added child.
- Making sure that the playdate is during a time when the child is not too hungry, too sleepy, or too overstimulated.
- Making sure that you will be able to pack a snack or lunch and accounting for whether the other child has allergies, because that will affect what you can pack for your child.
- Managing increased irritability or clinginess or whininess from the child if the playdate runs into a nap time.
- Managing any behavioral challenges that occur as the child is waking up (if the playdate is after a nap time)—also could include irritability, clinginess, or whininess.
- Adding the playdate to the calendar.
- Confirming with other parents the night before.
- Packing and preparing the child the day of the playdate.
- Going to the location.
- Dealing with socializing and any behavioral issues as they arise during the activity.

Table 10.3: Mental Load for Setting Up Playdate

Of course, you will not set up every playdate for your child, but on occasion you can do the whole process and know what to do for that to happen.

How about taking ownership of household tasks? If you are going to take ownership of a household task, it means you think about that task and know what it needs to be completed and whether you have the things to do it. If you don't, then you go buy them, and you do all the steps to it. Just like any other project. The major component is understanding that there is a necessary mental aspect before any visible actionable aspect can be made. Think about what the mental steps might be before the action is taken for it. What research, phone calls, emails, mental notes, or other thought processes might have to be done before you get to a place where you can do the thing you are thinking about?

After a lot of talking and honest communication with each other, Mark decides that he needs to show up better for Sandy in their relationship and take over a more equal share of the mental load. He isn't sure that he truly gets what the mental load is all about, so he decides to try to experience it by taking over the full responsibility for the care of one of their children.

During the communication, Mark and Sandy have come up with ways to make sure that they both have access to information so neither of them has to go through the other person to get to it anymore. Mark had always been taking full ownership of the finances, but now Sandy has access to a finance app that Mark uses to budget, so she can see how much is budgeted for every category, whether they are on budget or over, how much is left for the month, what is happening in savings, and how much is in their retirement accounts. Mark uses the app to do all the money moving and budget setting, and Sandy uses it solely to look in on the budget to keep transparency in that area. Finances should never be a secret in the relationship, as they can have detrimental effects on both people, even if one person is owning the responsibility for it. They are now using a shared electronic calendar on their phones, so when they each add something to it, they can see if there is anything else on the calendar already. They have agreed to include addresses, start and end times, and any important info in the notes section (like their week to bring the snack to soccer practice), and they turn on the calendar auto reminders to help them with the mental load. They also created a joint email account that has to do with anything child related or home related. They have agreed to each check that email at least once per day and to only delete an email after both have agreed that it is okay to delete it.

They are going to meet once per week now to check in with each other. This meeting will go over how things have gone for the week, what is going well, what kinks still need to be worked out, how they can support each other better, and small tasks like deleting emails. This check-in is scheduled to take less than thirty minutes, and as they get even more in sync and understand how to support each other and show up for each other, that will take less and less time.

Mark agrees to take ownership of the mental load and full responsibility for their eldest child for at least one year to get an idea of what the mental load is actually like by living it. He wants to try to remember all the things that Sandy usually remembers for him, like taking him to the doctor, buying him new clothes, registering him for soccer, getting him to friends' houses, taking him to birthday parties, helping him with his hygiene, getting him haircuts, dealing with the school, and managing summer activities. He also is agreeing to take on more of the responsibilities around the house and is taking ownership for certain chores and tasks that need to be done daily, weekly, and monthly. They sat down and went over all the things there are that have to be done to keep a house running smoothly, and then they picked and chose what they want to manage themselves out of their list until it felt like they had more equally distributed the list of responsibilities.

A few months after starting this egalitarian relationship, Mark seems nervous or distant in the evening one night. Their eldest child has been complaining that his ear has been hurting since Friday night, and it is now Sunday night and he is saying that it hurts so much that he can barely hear out of it. He is prone to getting ear infections, so Mark is thinking it is probably another ear infection. Mark and Sandy are getting into bed Sunday night, and Sandy is checking in with him.

SANDY: Mark, are you okay? You seem distant today, and I want to see if there is anything I can do to be there for you if something is going on.

MARK: Hmm. Oh, yeah. I'm fine. (He goes back into thought.)

SANDY: Mark, can you let me into your thoughts? Maybe I can just listen and hear what you are thinking about so heavily.

MARK: (Sighs. Sits down on the bed.) I have just been worried about Caleb and how he is not feeling well. I was trying to decide if I can wait until tomorrow, because the urgent cares are all closed and I don't think it is worthy of an ER visit, but if he can't sleep again tonight, then maybe it is, and I don't want his eardrum to burst or anything like that. If I take him in tomorrow morning, I can get us up and leave first thing when the urgent care opens up so that we are close to first in line. He probably has an ear infection, so I will have to run to the pharmacy and pick up an antibiotic for him and then get him back here before I can start to work. I will have to work from home tomorrow so if he needs anything I am available. So, just a lot of thoughts swirling around in my head on how best to take care of him and what that looks like for me for work tomorrow.

SANDY: Wow, sounds like a lot going on in your head right now.

MARK: Yeah . . . is this that mental load thing you were telling me about?

SANDY: This is a part of it. Yeah, I think you are experiencing it.

MARK: Ugh, this sucks. And I am only thinking about one thing. You do this kind of thinking but with multiple different thought processes going on at once?

SANDY: Yeah, I would have definitely expanded that and been thinking about even more there. I would have to think about how it affects their brother too. I would probably also be thinking about the kind of foods that Caleb will eat when he has an ear infection and checking to see if we have any soup, because if not, I would want to grab some at the store so that he will eat something tomorrow too.

MARK: Oh man, yeah, I forgot about that. This mental load thing is hard! I do not know how you have done it for all these years. I am sorry that I have not been more of an equal with you in this area, and I am definitely going to keep working on this so you are not alone in this anymore.

SANDY: Mark, that means so much to me to hear. Thank you. I appreciate all that you do and all that you are learning to do.

**REFLECTION 10.2: Equality in Responsibilities
for Unpaid Labor**

Do you consider yourself a traditional, transitional, or egalitarian? Why?

How often do you appreciate her for all that she does for your family?

How often do you expect appreciation for what you do around the home?

Is it equal? Do you expect more appreciation than you give? What changes can be made?

In what ways do you attempt to look for answers that you can find instead of going to her?

When you look at table 10.1, what part of the process would you be involved in or know about?

What are some ways that you and your partner can share information access more readily?

What are the tasks that need to be done around the house?

Which of those tasks would you consider taking ownership over?

How can you start a conversation with your partner to show you are willing to work toward an egalitarian relationship?

This ends our journey together, and I hope you have gained a lot from our time. This book is not all encompassing, obviously, but it is a starting point for you to begin your leveling-up experience. You will be able to practice what you have learned, and I also encourage you to seek out other places to continue learning.

I am including resources to start additional learning when you are ready. Remember that you can do this and that it takes practice, which means you will make mistakes and will have to start again. That is okay. Keep going. It will bring you closer to your partner, which helps you develop a better, more intimate connection, which certainly makes it more likely for you two to have more sexy-time experiences.

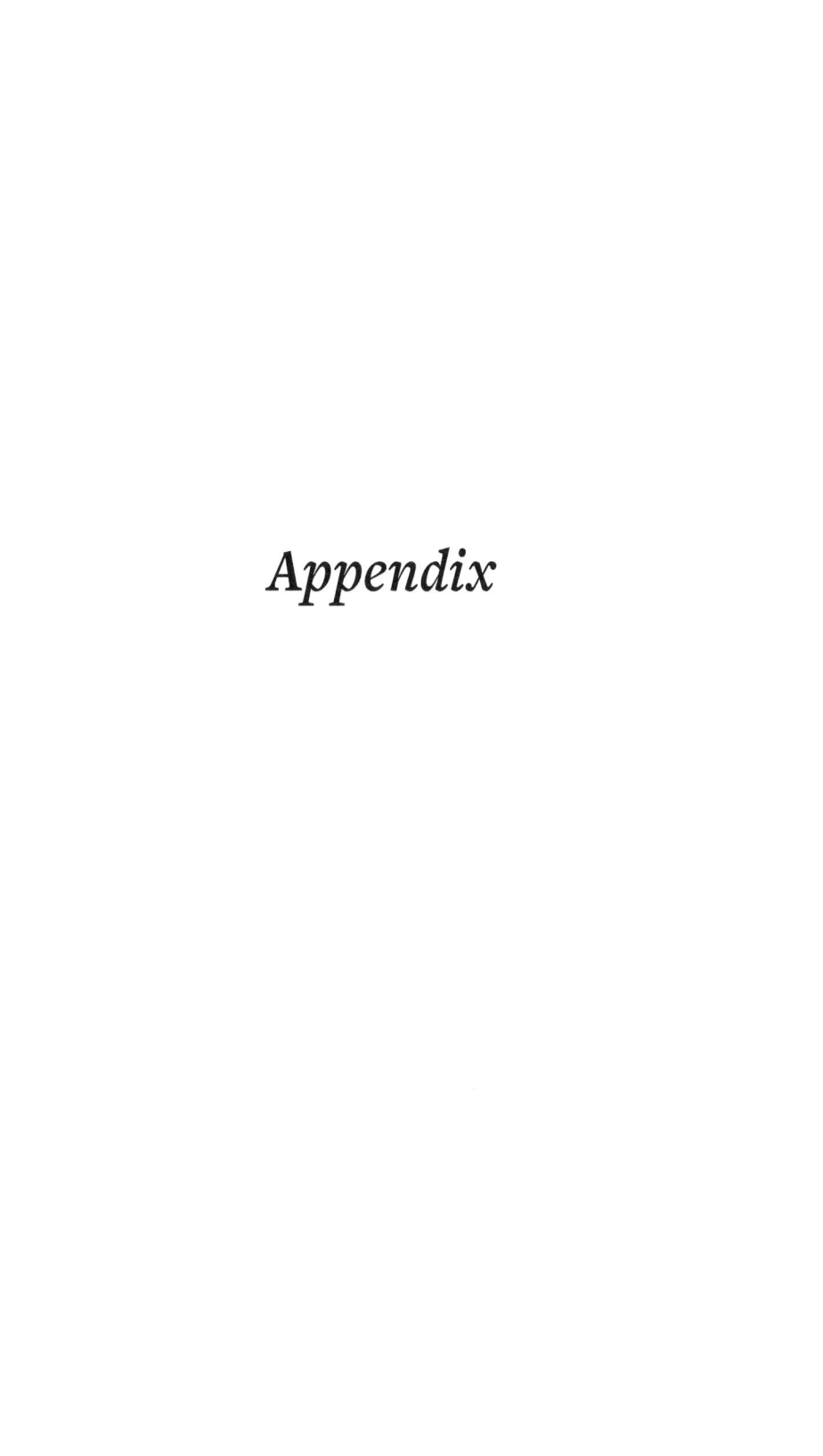

Appendix

Glossary of Terms (as used in this book)

Absolutist Language: Words that make it hard to regulate emotions and achieve goals, as they leave no room for times something happened outside of the absolute word. These words include *never, always,* and *constantly*. They set us up to not feel heard and push us apart instead of allowing us space to get closer together.

Cognitive Fatigue (Mental Fatigue): Overexertion of cognitive energy with executive functioning and mental load day in and day out for an extended period.

Communal: Relationship oriented, thinking about others and their needs instead of being focused solely on the self.

Communal Sexual Strength: Same as communal strength but with the focus on the sexual aspect of the relationship. Being responsive to times that sex is not of interest to a partner and being understanding of this need to find another way to connect intimately so relational and sexual satisfaction can remain high.

Communal Strength: Recognizing each other's needs and meeting them in a relationship instead of focusing only on your wants and needs. Having more give and take with a desire to make both partners satisfaction higher instead of the focus being on only one person.

Decision Fatigue: Another component of mental fatigue. Also a part of the executive functioning system, making decisions uses up limited space available in this system and can increase fatigue when the allocated space is full and a question is asked with a decision expected. Only so many conscious decisions can be made in a day before feeling decision fatigue and feeling unable to make any more decisions.

Egalitarian Relationships: Partners that are sharing the responsibilities for the family in a more equal way based on mutual respect for each other and each person's strengths, regardless of gender.

Executive Functioning: In the prefrontal cortex of the brain, this controls the neural processes necessary to regulate emotions, solve problems, make deliberate decisions, effectively plan, reflectively learn, and access working memory. It is how humans manage their working memory to successfully learn and manage life and where the mental load is used with planning memory, delegating, and reviewing.

Excessive Mental Demands in Mental Load: Unseen, invisible, and unpaid labor that is necessary for managing life and usually goes unnoticed by everyone except the person doing the mental work.

Groundhog Day Chores: Regularly repeating chores that are continuous and have no end, like laundry or the kitchen.

Inner Critic: Voice inside a person that tells them about their downfalls and how they screwed up throughout the day. It doesn't allow a person to be okay with being good enough; rather, it tells them how what they did could have been better and that they will never be good enough, which lowers their self-esteem.

Limerence Phase: The first six months to one year of a relationship. This involves the intense flood of emotions when you want to spend all your time with each other and are finding out all about each other. This is the time of the relationship where you are obsessed with each other.

Limited-Time-Only Chores: Chores that are able to be completed. Usually in a few minutes or happen only a limited number of times in a week, like taking out the trash or mowing the lawn.

Mental Load: Unpaid, domestic, invisible, caring, emotional, and mental labor that is constant, burdensome, and never-ending.

Mental Exhaustion: Fatigue that is continual and has now affected the ability to complete tasks, increased emotional stress, and decreased ability to regulate and manage self. There has not been enough rest to recover from fatigue, and they need help now. This exhaustion can lead to mental health issues like psychological distress, anxiety, and depression, along with feelings of dissatisfaction with life.

Prefrontal Cortex: Area of the brain that controls thoughts and behaviors that work together to allow people to make and accomplish goals and regulate themselves.

Self-compassion: How a person cares about themself. They show this by how they are kind versus self-critical, community versus isolation, mindfulness versus inner critic. When a person is high in self-compassion, they can give themself warmth during hard times versus if they have low self-compassion, when they will feel critical of themself as though the pain they are experiencing is deserved.

Self-esteem: How one feels about oneself. If it is high, then they believe they have value to other people and it helps them to be adaptive in situations, while on the other side, if it is low, then there tends to be a loss of confidence, high levels of depression, anxiety, poor mood, and less enjoyment of life.

Sexual Desire: An interest in sexual activity that brings a person to initiate or enthusiastically consent to receive their partner's initiation of sexual activity.

Sexual-Desire Discrepancy: When a couple's sexual desires do not match each other's and they feel it is a problem.

Sexy Time: A time to play and follow the pleasure with each other without any pressure to penetrate or orgasm for a goal. The only goal is to follow the pleasure and see where that takes you. A time to build sexual communal strength.

Unmitigated Sexual Communion: Total care for the other's needs and desires to the neglect of their own. This will have the opposite effect of communal strength.

Weaponized Incompetence: A strategy a person uses to avoid responsibility by passive-aggressively doing a task badly and then claiming that their partner is better at it or they don't understand how to do it well, even if they have been shown how to do it multiple times. It causes harm to the relationship because it creates an imbalance with the mental and emotional labors between the partners, as one person feels responsible for managing all parts of the family's life, including and mostly for childcare and housework, and the other person is able to do what they want without care.

Withdrawal of Affection: Conscious or unconscious consequence that comes from being told no to sex in particular but could be anything else that you wanted that includes pulling away (physically or emotionally), turning your back, leaving the room, withdrawing your hand, or becoming quiet.

Resources

Books

- *Fair Play: A Game-Changing Solution for When You Have Too Much to Do* by Eve Rodsky
- *I Didn't Sign Up for This: A Couples Therapist Shares Real-Life Stories of Breaking Patterns and Finding Joy in Relationships . . . Including Her Own* by Dr. Tracy Dalgleish
- *Fed Up: Emotional Labor, Women, and the Way Forward* by Gemma Hartley
- *The Time Has Come: Why Men Must Join the Gender Equality Revolution* by Michael Kaufman

Social Media Influencers

- Jimmy Knowles: attachment and mental load for men
- Zach Watson: mental load videos and coach for men

Podcasts

- *The Mental Load* by Katlynn Pyatt and Angie Cantrell
- *Take a Mental Load Off* by Rachel Gubler and Shauna Evans (specific to first responders, military members, and single parents)
- Do a podcast search for "mental load" to find episodes in other podcasts with great speakers talking about mental load.

References

Ahn, J. N., Haines, E. L., & Mason, M. F. (2017). "Gender Stereotypes and the Coordination of Mnemonic Work Within Heterosexual Couples: Romantic Partners Manage Their Daily To-Dos." *Sex Roles* 77(7–8), 435–452. https://doi.org/10.1007/s11199-017-0743-1

Anderson, E. (2023). "Hermeneutic Labor: The Gendered Burden of Interpretation in Intimate Relationships Between Women and Men." *Hypatia* 38(1), 177–197. https://doi.org/10.1017/hyp.2023.11

Balconi, M., Acconito, C., Allegretta, R. A., & Crivelli, D. (2023). "What Is the Relationship Between Metacognition and Mental Effort in Executive Functions? The Contribution of Neurophysiology." *Behavioral Sciences* 13(11), 918. https://doi.org/10.3390/bs13110918

Bataille, C. D., & Hyland, E. (2023). "Involved Fathering: How New Dads Are Redefining Fatherhood." *Personnel Review* 52(4), 1010–1032. https://doi.org/10.1108/PR-06-2019-0295

Bird, C. E. (1999). "Gender, Household Labor, and Psychological Distress: The Impact of the Amount and Division of Housework." *Journal of Health and Social Behavior* 40(1), 32–45. https://www.proquest.com/scholarly-journals/gender-household-labor-psychological-distress/docview/201661915/se-2

Bünning, M. (2020). "Paternal Part-Time Employment and Fathers' Long-Term Involvement in Child Care and Housework." *Journal of Marriage and Family* 82(2), 566–586. https://doi.org/10.1111/jomf.12608

Carlson, D. L., Miller, A. J., & Sassler, S. (2018). "Stalled for Whom? Change in the Division of Particular Housework Tasks and Their Consequences for Middle- to Low-Income Couples." *Socius: Sociological Research for a Dynamic World* 4(1–17). https://doi.org/10.1177/2378023118765867

Çevik, A. Ç., & Wright, G. (2023). "Hane İçi Karşılıksız Emeğin Zihinsel Yük Boyutu." [The Mental Load Dimension of Unpaid Household Labor] *Fe Dergi* 15(2), 50–83. https://doi.org/10.46655/federgi.1183599

Chen, Y., Fang, W., Guo, B., & Bau, H. (2021). "Fatigue-Related Effects in the Process of Task Interruption on Working Memory." *Frontiers in Human Neuroscience.* https://doi.org/10.3389/fnhum.2021.703422

Cherkasskaya, E., & Rosario, M. (2017). "A Model of Female Sexual Desire: Internalized Working Models of Parent-Child Relationships and Sexual Body Self-Representations." *Archives of Sexual Behavior* 46, 2429–2444. https://doi.org/10.1007/s10508-016-0899-8

Ciciolla, L., & Luthar, S. S. (2019). "Invisible Household Labor and Ramifications for Adjustment: Mothers as Captains of Households." *Sex Roles* 81(7–8), 467–486. https://doi.org/10.1007/s11199-018-1001-x

Dalgleish, T. (2023). *I Didn't Sign up for This: A Couples Therapist Shares Real-Life Stories of Breaking Patterns and Finding Joy in Relationships . . . Including Her Own.* Pesi Publishing Inc. ISBN-10 1683736621

Díaz-García, J., González-Ponce, I., Ponce-Bordòn, J. C., Lòpez-Gajardo, M. A., Ramírez-Bravo, I., Rubio-Morales, A., & García-Calvo, T. (2022). "Mental Load and Fatigue Assessment Instruments: A Systematic Review." *International Journal of Environmental Research and Public Health* 19(419). https://doi.org/10.3390/ijerph19010419

Diekman, A. B., Goodfriend, W., & Goodwin, S. (2004). "Dynamic Stereotypes of Power: Perceived Change and Stability in Gender Hierarchies." *Sex Roles* 50(3–4), 201–215. https://doi.org/10.1023/B:SERS.0000015552.22775.44

Dienberg, M., Oschatz, T., Piemonte, J. L., & Klein, V. (2023). "Women's Orgasm and Its Relationship with Sexual Satisfaction and Well-Being." *Current Sexual Health Reports* 15(3), 223–230. https://doi.org/10.1007/s11930-023-00371-0

Dinse, L., Adams, M., Vietta, C., Smith, A., Wilson, L., & Harris, S. (2023). "From Shame to Restoration: A Transformative Approach to Authentic Sexuality." *Social Work and Christianity* 50(2), 149–163. https://doi.org/10.3403/SWC.V50i2.361

Fahs, B., & Swank, E. (2017). "The Other Third Shift? Women's Emotion Work in Their Sexual Relationships." *Feminist*

Formations 28(3), 46–69. https://www.proquest.com/scholarly-journals/other-third-shift-womens-emotion-work-their/docview/1866465562/se-2

Fahs, B., Swank, E., & Shambe, A. (2020). "'I Just Go with It': Negotiating Sexual Desire Discrepancies for Women in Partnered Relationships." *Sex Roles* 83, 226–239. https://doi.org/10.1007/s11199-019-01098-w

Föyen, L. F., Sennerstam, V., Kontio, E., Lekander, M., Hedman-Lagerlöf, E., & Lindsäter, E. (2023). "Objective Cognitive Functioning in Patients with Stress-Related Disorders: A Cross-Sectional Study Using Remote Digital Cognitive Testing." *BMC Psychiatry* (23)565. https://doi.org/10.1186/s12888-023-05048-5

Gamble, R. S., Henry, J. D., & Vanman, E. J. (2023). "Empath Moderates the Relationship Between Cognitive Load and Prosocial Behavior." *Scientific Reports* 13, 824–834. https://doi.org/10.1038/s41598-023-28098-x

Gangal, A. D., R.N.M.Sc, Yigit, Y., & Ali, Y. (2024). Generational Differences in Attitudes towards Gender Roles and Violence Against Women. *International Journal of Caring Sciences,* 17(1), 198-208. https://www.proquest.com/scholarly-journals/generational-differences-attitudes-towards-gender/docview/3026158460/se-2

Girard, A. (2019). "Sexual Desire Discrepancy." *Current Sexual Health Reports* 11(2), 80–83. https://doi.org/10.1007/s11930-019-00196-w

Halie, W., & Harrison, K. (2021). "Interviews Exploring Emerging Adults' Everyday Life Gender Norm Experiences,

Media Gender Norm Perceptions, and Future Gender Norm Expectations." *Journal of Adult Development* 28(3), 207–220. https://doi.org/10.1007/s10804-020-09364-y

Hardies, K. (2022). "Normalising Gender Equality: Changing Gender Norms to Increase Gender Equality." *Tijdschrift Voor Genderstudies* 25(3), 212–230. https://doi.org/10.5117/TVGN2022.3.003.HARD

Harrington, E. E., & Reese-Melancon, C. (2022). "Who Is Responsible for Remembering? Everyday Prospective Memory Demands in Parenthood." *Sex Roles* 86(3–4), 189–207. https://doi.org/10.1007/s11199-021-01264-z

Harris, E. A., Gormezano, A. M., & van Anders, S. M. (2022). "Gender Inequities in Household Labor Predict Lower Sexual Desire in Women Partnered with Men." *Archives of Sexual Behavior* 51(8), 3847–3870. https://doi.org/10.1007/s10508-022-02397-2

Hax, C. (2024, Jul. 15). "It's My husband's Turn to Be Class Parent—So Why Am I Doing the Work Again?" *The Washington Post.* https://www.proquest.com/newspapers/my-husbands-turn-be-class-parent-so-why-am-i/docview/3080013226/se-2

Hogue, J. V., Rosen, N. O., Bockaj, A., Impett, E. A., & Muise, A. (2019). "Sexual Communal Motivation in Couples Coping with Low Sexual Interest/Arousal: Associations with Sexual Well-Being and Sexual Goals." *PLoS One* 14(7). https://doi.org/10.1371/journal.pone.0219768

Holas, P., Kowalczyk, M., Krejtz, I., Wisiecka, K., & Jankowski, T. (2023). "The Relationship Between Self-Esteem and

Self-Compassion in Socially Anxious: Research and Reviews." *Current Psychology* 42(12), 10271–10276. https://doi.org/10.1007/s12144-021-02305-2

Huntsinger, J. R., & Raoul, A. (2022). "Only as a Last Resort: Sociocultural Differences Between Women and Men Explain Women's Heightened Reaction to Threat, Not Evolutionary Principles." *Behavioral and Brain Sciences* 45. https://doi.org/10.1017/S0140525X22000516

Imhoff, R., & Hoffmann, L. (2023). "Prenatal Sex Role Stereotypes: Gendered Expectations and Perceptions of (Expectant) Parents." *Archives of Sexual Behavior* 52(3), 1095–1104. https://doi.org/10.1007/s10508-023-02584-9

Impett, E. A., Muise, A., & Rosen, N. O. (2015). "Is It Good to Be Giving in the Bedroom? A Prosocial Perspective on Sexual Health and Well-Being in Romantic Relationships." *Current Sexual Health Reports* 7(3), 180–190. https://doi.org/10.1007/s11930-015-0055-9

Jessee, A., Mangelsdorf, S. C., Wong, M. S., Schoppe-Sullivan., S. J., Shigeto, A., & Brown, G. L. (2018). "The Role of Reflective Functioning in Predicting Marital and Coparenting Quality." *Journal of Child and Family Studies* 27, 187–197. https://doi.org/10.1007/s10826-017-0874-6

Johnson, S., & Zuccarini, D. (2010). "Integrating Sex and Attachment in Emotionally Focused Couple Therapy." *Journal of Marital and Family Therapy* 36(4), 431–445. https://doi.org/10.1111/j.1752-0606.2009.00155.x

Johri, M. (2023). "Feminist Perspective on Patriarchy: Its Impact on the Construction of Femininity and Masculinity."

New Literaria 4(2), 1–9. https://doi.org/10.48189/nl.2023. v04i2.001

Kalmbach, D. A., Fernandez-Mendoza, J., & Drake, C. L. (2023). "Stress and Sleep Reactivity Increase Risk for Insomnia: Highlighting the Dynamic Interplay Between Sleep-Wake Regulation and Stress Responsivity." *Sleep* 46(2). https://doi. org/10.1093/sleep/zsac302

Kalyuga, S. (2011). "Cognitive Load Theory: How Many Types of Load Does It Really Need?" *Educational Psychology Review* 23, 1–19. https://doi.org/10.1007/s10648-010-9150-7

Klusmann, P. D. (2002). "Sexual Motivation and the Duration of Partnership." *Archives of Sexual Behavior* 31(3), 275–287.

La Rochebrochard, E., & Rozée, V. (2022). "Revealing Gender Double Standards in the Parenthood Norm Depends on Question Order." *Sex Roles* 86(7–8), 471–481. https://doi. org/10.1007/s11199-022-01276-3

Macedo, A., Capela, E, & Peixoto, M. (2023). "Sexual Satisfaction Among Lesbian and Heterosexual Cisgender Women: A Systematic Review and Meta-Analysis." *Healthcare* (11)1680. https://doi.org/10.3390.healthcare11121680

Mark, K. P. (2014). "The Impact of Daily Sexual Desire and Daily Sexual Desire Discrepancy on the Quality of the Sexual Experience in Couples." *Canadian Journal of Human Sexuality* 23(1), 27–33. https://doi.org/10.3138/cjhs.23.1.A2

McConnon, A., Midgette, A. J., & Conry-Murray, C. (2022). "Mother Like Mothers and Work Like Fathers: U.S. Heterosexual College Students' Assumptions About Who

Should Meet Childcare and Housework Demands." *Sex Roles* 86(1–2), 49–66. https://doi.org/10.1007/s11199-021-01252-3

McGarity-Shipley, E., Eun-Young, L., & Pyke, K. E. (2023). "A Pilot Cross-Sectional Investigation of Chronic Shame as a Mediator of the Relationship Between Subjective Social Status and Self-Rated Health Among Middle-Aged Adults." *Health Psychology and Behavioral Medicine* 11(1). https://doi.org /10.1080/21642850.2023.2268697

McLean, C., Musolino, C., Rose, A., & Ward, P. R. (2023). "The Management of Cognitive Labour in Same-Gender Couples." *PLoS One* 18(7). https://doi.org/10.1371/journal.pone.0287585

Mercurio, A. E., & Landry, L. J. (2008). "Self-Objectification and Well-Being: The Impact of Self-Objectification on Women's Overall Sense of Self-Worth and Life Satisfaction." *Sex Roles* 58, 458–466. https://doi.org/10.1007/s11199-007-9357-3

Minamoto, T., Shipstead, Z., Osaka, N., & Engle, R. W. (2015). "Low Cognitive Load Strengthens Distractor Interference While High Load Attenuates When Cognitive Load and Distractor Possess Similar Visual Characteristics." *Atten Percept Psychophys* 77, 1659–1673. https://doi.org/10.3758/ s13414-015-0866-9

Muise, A. (2017). "When and for Whom Is Sex Most Beneficial? Sexual Motivation in Romantic Relationships." *Canadian Psychology* 58(1), 69–74. https://doi.org/10.1037/cap0000094

Ohlsson-Wijk, S., Brandén, M., & Duvander, A. (2022). "Getting Married in a Highly Individualized Context: Commitment and Gender Equality Matter." *Journal of Marriage and Family* 84(4), 1081–1104. https://doi.org/10.1111/jomf.12849

Parfenova, A., & Kozlova, M. (2023). "The Regulatory Power of Social Expectations: Developing a Measurement Scale." *The International Journal of Sociology and Social Policy* 43(5), 569–585. https://doi.org/10.1108/IJSSP-06-2022-0139

Pitts, R. T. (2023). "MAMA SCHOLARSHIP: Tackling the Motherlode." *Curriculum and Teaching Dialogue* 25(1), 291–295, 342. https://www.proquest.com/scholarly-journals/mama-scholarship-tackling-motherlode/docview/2866471635/se-2

Raposo, S., Impett, E. A., & Muise, A. (2020). "Avoidantly Attached Individuals Are More Exchange-Oriented and Less Communal in the Bedroom." *Archives of Sexual Behavior* 49(8), 2863–2881. https://doi.org/10.1007/s10508-020-01813-9

Rathner, S. (2024, Apr. 19). "How Couples Can Share the Mental Load of Money Management." *The Times-Tribune.* https://www.proquest.com/newspapers/how-couples-can-share-mental-load-money/docview/3041457430/se-2

Rodsky, E. (2019). *Fair Play: A Game Changing Solution for When You Have Too Much to Do (and More Life to Live).* New York. G.P. Putnam's Sons. ISBN: 9780525541936

Rutherford, H. J. V., Byrne, S. P., Crowley, M. J., Bornstein, J., Bridgett, D. J., & Mayes, L. C. (2018). "Executive Functioning Predicts Predictive Functioning in Mothers." *Journal of Child and Family Studies* 27, 944–952. https://doi.org/10.1007/s10826-017-0928-9

Sævik, K. W., & Konijnenberg, C. (2023). "The Effects of Sexual Shame, Emotion Regulation and Gender on Sexual

Desire." *Scientific Reports* 13:4042. https://doi.org/10.1038/s41598-023-31181-y

Salomone, M., Burle, B., Fabre, L., & Berberian, B. (2021). "An Electromyographic Analysis of the Effects of Cognitive Fatigue on Online and Anticipatory Action Control." *Frontiers in Human Neuroscience* (14)615046. https://doi.org/10.3389/fnhum.2020.615046

Sarmiento, M. I., Hwang, J., & Midgette, A. J. (2024). "'The Children Don't Do Enough': Including Children in Fairness Perceptions of Housework." *Journal of Marriage and Family* 86(2), 433–454. https://doi.org/10.1111/jomf.12966

Shelton, B. A., & John, D. (1996). "The Division of Household Labor." *Annual Review of Sociology* 22, 299–322. https://www.proquest.com/scholarly-journals/division-household-labor/docview/199596419/se-2

Schilperoort, L. (2021). "Striving Towards Equal Partnerships: Church-Going Couples and the Division of Household-Related Mental Labour." *New Zealand Sociology* 36(1), 77–101. https://www.proquest.com/scholarly-journals/striving-towards-equal-partnerships-church-going/docview/2593906802/se-2

Sutherland, S. E., Rehman, U. S., Fallis, E. E., & Goodnight, J. A. (2015). "Understanding the Phenomenon of Sexual Desire Discrepancy in Couples." *The Canadian Journal of Human Sexuality* 24(2), 141–150. https://doi.org/10/3138/cjhs.242.A3

Tammelin, M. (2021). "Couples' Time Management Systems: Your Time, My Time or Our Time?" *Families, Relationships and Societies* 10(1), 137–152. https://doi.org/10.1332/204674 320X16059402201264

Træen, B., & Kvalem, I. L. (2023). "The Longer It Is, the Closer One Feels: Perception of Emotional Closeness to the Partner, Relationship Duration, Sexual Activity, and Satisfaction in Married and Cohabiting Persons in Norway." *Sexuality & Culture* 27(3), 761–785. https://doi.org/10.1007/s12119-022-10037-z

Trujillo, L. T. (2019). "Mental Effort and Information-Processing Costs Are Inversely Related to Global Brain Free Energy During Visual Categorization." *Frontiers in Neuroscience* 13(1292). https://doi.org/10.3389/fnins.2019.01292

Tuohy, W. (2022). "Mental Load Is a Mother Load: Exclusive." *The Age*. Fairfax Media Publications. https://www.proquest.com/newspapers/mental-load-is-mother/docview/2676909391/se-2?accountid=205336

Vowels, L. M., & Mark, K. P. (2020). "Strategies for Mitigating Sexual Desire Discrepancy in Relationships." *Archives of Sexual Behavior* 49, 1017–1028. https://doi.org/10.1007/s10508-020-1640-y

Vowels, L. M., Roos, C. A., Mehulić, J., O'Dean, S. M., & Sánchez-Hernández, M. D. (2022). "What Does It Mean to Be Responsive to a Partner's Sexual Needs? Toward a Definition of Sexual Need Responsiveness." *Archives of Sexual Behavior* 51(8), 3735–3747. https://doi.org/10.1007/s10508-022-02432-2

Walker, A. M., & Lutmer, A. (2023). "Caring, Chemistry, and Orgasms: Components of Great Sexual Experiences." *Sexuality & Culture* 27(5), 1735–1756. https://doi.org/10.1007/s12119-023-10087-x

Wetzel, G. M., Cultice, R. A., & Sanchez, D. T. (2022). "Orgasm Frequency Predicts Desire and Expectation for Orgasm: Assessing the Orgasm Gap Within Mixed-Sex Couples." *Sex Roles* 86(7–8), 456–470. https://doi.org/10.1007/s11199-022-01280-7

Wilton, E. P., Gladstone, T. R., Luke, A. L., Brennan, E., & Flessner, C. (2021). "The Relationship between Parent Executive Functioning and Accommodation." *Journal of Child and Family Studies* 32, 314–332. https://doi.org/10.1007/s10826-021-02155-3

Wojciechowska, M. (2023). "'I Was Ashamed, and Now I Am Proud as I Finally Know How to Let Go.' How Female Polers Perceive, Experience, and Give Meanings to Their Bodies—An Ethnographic Case Study." *Qualitative Sociology Review* 19(4) https://www.proquest.com/scholarly-journals/i-was-ashamed-now-am-proud-as-finally-know-how/docview/2913314229/se-2

Wong, B. (2022, Jan. 28). "'Weaponized Incompetence' Screws Women Over at Work and in Relationships." *Yerepouni Daily News.* https://www.proquest.com/newspapers/weaponized-incompetence-screws-women-over-at-work/docview/2623269737/se-2

Yatziv, T., Kessler, Y., & Atzaba-Poria, N. (2018). "What's Going On in My Baby's Mind? Mother's Executive Functions Contribute to Individual Differences in Maternal Mentalization During Mother-Infant Interactions." *PLoS One* 13(11) e0207869. https://doi.org10.1371/journal.pone.0207869

Yoo, J., Slavish, D., Dietch, J. R., Kelly, K., Ruggero, C., & Taylor, D. J. (2023). "Daily Reactivity to Stress and Sleep Disturbances:

Unique Risk Factors for Insomnia." *Sleep* 46(2). https://doi.org/10.1093/sleep/zsac256

Zainal, N. H., & Newman, M. G. (2022). "A Cross-Lagged Prospective Network Analysis of Depression and Anxiety and Cognitive Functioning Components in Midlife Community Adult Women." *Psychological Medicine* 53, 4160–4171. https://doi.org/10.1017/S0033291722000848

About the Author

Dr. Celeste McClannahan is a compassionate voice in the world of relationships and emotional healing. A licensed Marriage and Family Therapist (LMFT) with a PhD in Clinical Sexology, she has helped hundreds of individuals and couples navigate the complexities of connection, communication, and intimacy. Drawing on clinical expertise, personal insight, and deep empathy, she brings clarity to the often-invisible burdens that impact emotional and sexual connection in heterosexual relationships, offering a safe and affirming space for clients of all identities.

In *Room in Her Head*, Dr. Celeste offers the first comprehensive guide written specifically for men to understand mental load, how it affects sexual desire, and how to become a more egalitarian partner. Her work is grounded in real conversations from the therapy room, and fueled by her passion for building fresh, safe, and secure relationships—where partners communicate better, navigate challenges more smoothly, and create a new relationship that feels stronger and more connected.

When she's not in session, Celeste enjoys the natural beauty of Washington State, laughing with her family, and deepening her own relationships—with joy and intentionality.